Plate & Palette

A Collection of Fine Art and Food from Beaufort County, North Carolina

The intent of the Cookbook Committee is to paint a picture of life in Beaufort County, pictorially and gastronomically. We hope your journey through this book will provide just that.

The Beaufort County Arts Council has included in this collection favorite recipes taken from the personal files of its supporters and friends, and has no reason to doubt that the ingredients and instructions are accurate. The recipes in this book were submitted by a variety of sources, and neither Beaufort County Arts Council nor the contributors, publisher, printer, distributors, or sellers of this volume are responsible for errors, omissions, or degrees of recipe success.

We regret that **Plate & Palette** was unable to include all of the recipes submitted due to similarity or space constraints.

Copyright 2001 by Beaufort County Arts Council

ISBN 0-9709549-0-5

1st Printing	3,000	September 2001
2nd Printing	1,500	December 2002

Copies of **Plate & Palette** may be obtained by sending $25.00 (tax included) plus $5.00 shipping and handling to the following address. For your convenience, order forms are located in the back of the cookbook.

Beaufort County Arts Council
108 Gladden Street
P.O. Box 634
Washington, NC 27889
252-946-2504

e-mail: beauxarts@coastalnet.com
website: www.beaufortcountyartscouncil.org

*Front cover art – **After the Storm** by Don Miller*

*Back cover art – **Is the Ferry Coming?** by Sally Hofmann*

Cover concept and cookbook design by Lauren Kay Sinclair Designs, Blounts Creek, NC

WIMMER
COOKBOOKS

ConsolidatedGraphics

1-800-548-2537

Table of Contents

Plate & Palette

Keeping the 'Arts Alive'

Thank you for buying this cookbook and making an investment in the future of the arts in Beaufort County.

Proceeds from its sale will help fund *Arts Alive*, the Beaufort County Arts Council's newly-created endowment. This will be a permanent source of funding that will enable the Arts Council to continue to fulfill its mission of providing diverse cultural opportunities in Beaufort County and to be a moving force in the area's involvement in the arts.

Arts Alive is a designated fund, under the umbrella of the Beaufort County chapter of the North Carolina Community Foundation, which will enable donors to benefit the Arts Council with their charitable donations. The Arts Council hopes to establish an endowment of between $500,000 and $1 million, with the interest being used to defray the agency's annual operating and program costs and to help secure operating funds for the Arts Council that will be managed through the North Carolina Community Foundation.

The Arts Council provides frequently changing exhibits of area artists' visual works (paintings, photography, pottery, mixed media) in the Washington Civic Center gallery on weekdays from 9 a.m. to 4 p.m. The Arts Council also operates the Lane Gift Shop that features works by local artists and artisans at its offices located in the restored Atlantic Coast Line train depot in downtown Washington.

The Arts Council also promotes the arts in the local schools by sponsoring a series of cultural programs for school children throughout Beaufort County.

Arts Council events are open to the public throughout the year.

First South Bank Art Collection

The works of art featured in this cookbook are part of the First South Bank art collection. The collection began in 1976 after Tom Vann, president of First South Bank (then Home Savings and Loan), developed a keen interest in the visual arts during his work as facilities chairman for Beaufort County Arts Council's event "ARTRAIN."

Through his work and with the advice of longtime arts advocate Louise Lane, Mr. Vann and the savings and loan's board of directors decided to begin buying art for the office. There were two constraints placed on these purchases: the art would be produced by eastern North Carolina artists, and no more than two works by any one artist would be purchased for the collection.

For the most part, the collection has met these criteria during the last 25 years. As the bank grew, its art collection has grown - from a single purchase in 1976, to more than 530 art works in all media and all styles. Today, the collection includes everything from traditional oil portraits of eastern North Carolinians in their everyday lives to abstract sculptures and weavings.

In acquiring its art collection, First South Bank not only has enhanced the lives of its customers and employees but also has become one of the major buyers at eastern North Carolina art shows, thereby encouraging artists throughout the region. As of March 2001, the artists currently or formerly residing in Beaufort County who are represented in the First South Bank collection include:

Walter Alligood	Pat Holscher	Mildred Rumley
Linda Boyer	*Jeffrey Jakub	Alice Stallings
*Betty Bonner Bradshaw	Sandra Jones	Amanda Toler
Betty Bracy	*Diane Lee	*Frans van Baars
Mark Collis	*Don Miller	*Dorothy Anne Walker
Nancy Collis	*Lyn Mallison Morrow	Jayne Davis Wall
Betty Crompton	Sharon H. Muir	*Sam Wall III
*Irene Glover Forbes	*Riley Potts Simpson	Sears Wolff
Anita Franklin	Sally Raulerson	Gary Ray Woolard
Barbara J. Hardy	Joanna Register	*Roberta Woolridge
Gray Hodges	*Anne M. Respess	
*Sally Hofmann	Ruth Rose	

Asterisk denotes Beaufort County artist in book

For more information on artists, please contact Beaufort County Arts Council at beauxarts@coastalnet.com

Plate & Palette

Beaufort County Arts Council Cookbook Committee

Co-Chairs

Louise Lane   Jane Page

Steering Committee Members

Olivia Roberson
Sue Nicholson
Laura Bell
Anne Stuart Rumley

Charlene B. Alligood
Sarah Sloan
Leah Pyburn
Sandra Harvey

Jackie Everett, Technical Advisor
Lauren Sinclair, Graphic Designer

Heritage Committee

Athy Cooper
Sadie Fowle
Nan Hawkins

Editorial Committee

Sue Nicholson
Marilyn Roth
Betty Anne Dicken
Ann Peters

Publicity

Beaufort County Arts Council Staff
Betty Mitchell Gray
Helen Sommerkamp
Kay Currie

Fundraising

Laura Bell
Marilyn Roth

Marketing

Alice McClure

Members-at-Large

Leonard and Johanna Huber
Jane Fields
Dianne and Bill Castle
Margaret Dorn
Muriel Brothers
Georgia O'Farrow
Sue Radcliffe
Lexa Upton
Ardis Messick Hatch
Florence Lodge
Ann Windley
Kaye Mayer
Barbara Voliva
Jan De Hoog
Roberta Woolridge
Becky Tuten
Mary Alice Chapin
Ann Darkow

The Committee thanks all those others throughout the county who helped us in any way. We also thank Wanda Johnson, Director of the Beaufort County Arts Council, and the staff who worked tirelessly with us.

Plate & Palette

Ann M. Respess

*Getting Supper by
the Bridge*

watercolor

Appetizers & Beverages

Election Night Dip

2   (8-ounce) packages cream cheese
2   (16-ounce) cans black beans, drained
1   large onion, chopped
1   jar raspberry salsa (available in upscale grocery spots - a must!)
2   packages pepper jack cheese, grated (Kraft brand)

Soften cream cheese and spread in oven-proof dish. Layer with black beans, chopped onion, raspberry salsa, and pepper jack cheese. Bake in preheated oven at 350 degrees for about 30 minutes, or until cheese is well-melted and bubbly. Serve with tortilla chips…the lime flavored are the best!

Marcia Griffin
Washington

Artichoke Dip

1   cup mayonnaise
1   can unmarinated artichoke hearts, drained and chopped
1   cup grated sharp cheddar cheese
1   teaspoon basil
2   garlic cloves, minced

Mix all ingredients. Put in 9x13-inch baking dish and bake at 350 degrees for 20 to 30 minutes.

This can be baked about 20 minutes and reheated the next day. Sourdough round bread loaves can be hollowed out and used for bowls, reserving the pieces of bread for dipping, or serve with crackers.

Roberta Woolridge
Belhaven

Celery-Honey Fruit Dip

I love to serve this with a big bowl of beautiful strawberries!

1/2	cup sugar
1	teaspoon dry mustard
1	teaspoon paprika
1/4	teaspoon salt
1/3	cup honey
1	tablespoon lemon juice
1/4	cup vinegar
1	cup vegetable oil
1	teaspoon grated onion
1	teaspoon celery seed

Combine first 7 ingredients in a blender or food processor. Blend well. Slowly add oil, continuing to blend until thick. Stir in onion and celery seed. Cover and store in refrigerator.

Yield: 1 3/4 cups

Anne Stuart Rumley
Washington

Bell Pepper Dip

2	eggs, beaten
2	tablespoons sugar
2	tablespoons vinegar
2	tablespoons butter
2	(3-ounce) packages cream cheese (or one 8-ounce package), room temperature
1/2	medium onion, chopped
1/2	green bell pepper, chopped

Cook first 4 ingredients over medium heat, stirring constantly, until thick. Cool. Cream together cooked mixture and cream cheese. Stir in chopped onion and pepper. Serve at room temperature with round, buttery crackers.

Grace Bonner
Aurora

Spicy Clam Dip

1	(3-ounce) package cream cheese, softened
1	tablespoon sour cream
2	tablespoons fresh lemon juice
2	teaspoons Worcestershire sauce
1	teaspoon grated onion
1	teaspoon horseradish
1	tablespoon chili sauce
	pinch of salt
1	(7 1/2-ounce) can minced clams, well-drained

Blend cream cheese with sour cream. Stir in remaining ingredients. Serve as a dip for potato chips, club crackers or raw vegetables.

Yield: Approximately 2 cups

Elizabeth Holmes
Washington

Lind Graves' Shrimp Dip

1	pound shrimp, cooked and deveined
1	(8-ounce) package cream cheese, softened
3/4	cup mayonnaise
	salt
	ground white or red pepper
2	lemons, juiced
3	tablespoons ketchup
1	small onion, grated

Chop shrimp. Grate onion. Combine softened cream cheese and mayonnaise, salt and red pepper. Add shrimp and mix well. Chill and serve.

Yield: 12 servings

Lind Graves
Washington

Serve with crackers and be sure to make plenty…it will go fast. I make this for every party we have and it is a favorite of everyone.

Vidalia Onions on Crackers

5 to 6	medium Vidalia onions, sliced in rings and cut in half
1	cup water
1/2	cup sugar
1/4	cup vinegar
2	tablespoons celery seed
	mayonnaise

Bring water, sugar, vinegar and celery seed to a boil in a large saucepan. Add onions, return to a boil making sure all onions are covered with liquid. Cover and remove from heat. Leave for 15 to 20 minutes. Drain. When onions have cooled, coat with mayonnaise and serve with mild crackers.

Jan Sparrow
Washington

Black Olive Salsa

2	(4-ounce) cans black olives, drained and chopped
1	(4-ounce) can chopped green chiles, drained (you decide on the heat)
3 to 5	medium tomatoes, chopped
3 to 5	green onions, chopped
3	tablespoons olive oil
1 1/2	tablespoons red wine vinegar
1/8	teaspoon garlic salt
	dash of pepper

We love this in the summer served over grilled tuna.

Combine all ingredients and chill overnight. Serve with tortilla chips.

Jeff Rumley
Washington

Tapenade

3/4   cup chopped kalamata or black olives
1   tablespoon finely chopped capers
3   tablespoons finely chopped anchovies
1   tablespoon finely chopped garlic
1   tablespoon finely chopped shallots
      juice of 1/2 lemon
1/4   cup olive oil
      Piri Piri Sauce

Mix ingredients together. Serve on toasted baguette slices drizzled with some piri piri sauce.

Linda Niederbuehl
Washington

Piri Piri Sauce

1/3   cup olive oil
1/2   cup chopped jalapeño peppers
1   tablespoon cayenne, or to taste
1   teaspoon salt
1/2   teaspoon black pepper
1/4   cup minced garlic

Heat all ingredients, except garlic, in saucepan. Simmer for 30 minutes and cool. Put all ingredients into blender and blend until smooth. Keeps indefinitely in refrigerator, but it's best when allowed to age a couple of weeks.

Linda Niederbuehl
Washington

Excellent sauce on shrimp or pork.

Szechuan Green Beans

1 to 2 pounds fresh green beans, slightly cooked beyond blanching

Mix in casserole:

2 to 3 garlic cloves, minced
1 inch ginger root, chopped finely
2 tablespoons soy sauce
1 teaspoon dark sesame oil
3 teaspoons rice wine vinegar

Add green beans and marinate for a couple of hours before serving at room temperature.

Sue Mansfield
Washington

Great hors d'oeuvre, using toothpicks or fingers!

Tortellini Platter

1 package tri-colored cheese tortellini
1 package Knorr pesto mix, prepared (follow directions on package)
2 (8-ounce) packages cream cheese, softened
2 tablespoons lemon juice
  green pepper, cut into strips
  red pepper, cut into strips
  assortment of black olives and Spanish olives

Mixed prepared pesto with cream cheese and lemon juice. Serve dip with cooked tortellini, pepper strips and olives. Makes a very attractive platter.

Judy Lewis
Washington

Spinach Balls

2	(10-ounce) boxes frozen chopped spinach, thawed
1 1/2	large sweet onions
5	well-beaten eggs
1/2	cup grated Parmesan cheese
1/2	teaspoon thyme
1	tablespoon Accent
2	cups herb-seasoned stuffing mix
3/4	cup butter or margarine, melted
1 to 3	teaspoons garlic salt, to taste
1	teaspoon pepper

Put onions in food processor and process until onions are a grated consistency. Add eggs. Add cheese, thyme, Accent, garlic salt and pepper. Mix the well-drained spinach and herb dressing in with egg mixture and add the melted butter. Use a heaping teaspoon to measure the amount to form balls. Bake at 350 degrees for 15 minutes.

Yield: 40 balls

Diane Geis
Chocowinity

Chopped broccoli may be used in place of spinach. Red pepper, curry, red pepper sauce or jalapeño all purpose seasoning can be added for a little zing. Experiment!

Hilda's Tea Treats

3/4	cup shelled and finely chopped pistachio nuts
1	(8-ounce) package cream cheese, room temperature
2 to 3	tablespoons butter, softened
	pinch of salt
2	(11-ounce) cans Mandarin oranges, drained
1	loaf very thin sliced white bread

Flatten bread slices with rolling pin and with two-inch biscuit cutter, cut two circles from each slice of bread. Soften cream cheese to spreadable consistency, using two to three tablespoons of softened butter. Assemble sandwiches by spreading bread circle with cream cheese, placing a Mandarin orange slice in center of circle. Fold into crescent, pinching ends slightly. Spread cream cheese on crescent edges. Dip into pistachio nuts.

Yield: Approximately 50 sandwiches

Marilyn Roth
Washington

An unusual, bite-size sandwich that stars at high teas.

A superb cook, Hilda was gracious with her left-overs. If the Metropolitan Opera was in town, Lobster Thermidor came my way since she prepared the delicious food for the après-opera buffets. Never did give me that recipe, but she encouraged me to learn to cook and to explore the many cuisines of the world.

Pickled Mushrooms

2/3   cup red wine vinegar
2/3   cup salad oil
1   medium onion, thinly sliced, separated into rings
1 1/2 teaspoons salt
2   tablespoons fresh parsley (or 1 tablespoon dried)
1   teaspoon prepared mustard
1   tablespoon brown sugar
1/2   teaspoon each thyme, oregano and garlic powder
1   pound fresh mushrooms (or 2 6-ounce cans)

In small saucepan combine all ingredients except mushrooms, bring to boil. Pour into container, add mushrooms, cover and chill several hours. Drain to serve. Use toothpicks or cocktail forks.

Johanna and Leonard Huber
Washington

Mary Beth's Caramelized Bacon-Wrapped Breadsticks

Grissini is the Italian word for breadsticks. Authentic grissini are very thin, making them perfect for this recipe. Look for them in the cracker or bread section of the supermarket.

1   package breadsticks, approximately 9 ounces
2   (1-pound) packages bacon
1/2   cup dark brown sugar, firmly packed
1   teaspoon cumin
1   teaspoon chili powder
1/8   teaspoon cayenne pepper

Mix sugar, cumin, chili powder and cayenne together in a small bowl. Place mixture in a shallow dish. Roll a bacon strip tightly around each breadstick. Next, roll breadstick in sugar mixture, coating heavily and place seam-side down on a parchment-lined baking sheet. Broil until bacon is crispy.

Yield: 24 wrapped breadsticks

Beth Collier
Washington

Mushroom Bacon Roll-ups

2 1/2	large loaves white bread
3	sticks butter
2	large onions, chopped
1 1/2	pounds chopped mushrooms
2	(8-ounce) packages cream cheese
1	tablespoon sherry, to taste (optional)
1/2	pound bacon
10	drops Tabasco sauce
	salt and pepper to taste
	paprika

As this is a time-consuming recipe, it helps to make the mushroom mixture on one day and then do the roll-ups in the next day or two. The roll-ups can be cut and frozen for several months.

Remove bread crusts with a bread knife and roll each slice of crustless bread with a rolling pin until flattened. Sauté onions in 1 stick of melted butter and add mushrooms, sautéing briefly. Add cream cheese to mushrooms and stir until melted. Add sherry if desired. Microwave the bacon until crisp. Crumble the bacon into the mushroom mixture. Add the Tabasco and salt and pepper to taste. Spread a thin layer of the mushroom mixture on a flattened piece of bread. Roll up in a jelly roll fashion and dip the roll-ups in the remainder of the melted butter (about 2 sticks). Repeat these steps until mushroom mixture is gone. Sprinkle the mushroom roll-ups with paprika and garlic powder and cut each roll into four bite size pieces. Bake in a preheated 400 degree oven for 10 to 20 minutes.

Yield: Approximately 200 pieces

Sue M. Nicholson
Bath

Cheese and Almond Strips

1	loaf very thin sliced white bread, crusts removed
1/2	pound cheddar cheese, shredded
6	slices bacon, cooked crisp and crumbled
2 to 3	tablespoons very finely chopped onion
3/4	cup chopped almonds, lightly toasted
1	cup real mayonnaise
2	teaspoons Worcestershire sauce

My very favorite!

Mix all above ingredients. Spread on bread. Cut each slice into three strips. (At this point, a cookie sheet full may be frozen and then stored in freezer bags to have "hot" hors d'oeuvres on hand for impromptu entertaining.) When ready to serve, bake at 400 degrees for 10 to 12 minutes.

Kaye Mayer
Washington

Cheese Daisies

Around 1950, my mother, Katie Harding, saw this recipe by Ann Batchelor in Ladies' Home Journal and began making them. When she lost her sight, she asked me, to make them. I sold them for $1 a hundred.

2	sticks butter
1	stick oleo (not soft-spread)
1/2	cup grated Parmesan cheese
1	pound extra sharp cheddar cheese
1	teaspoon salt
4	cups all-purpose flour
1	teaspoon cayenne pepper

Cream butter and oleo well. Add Parmesan cheese and continue to cream until light. Grate cheddar cheese with Mouli grater, add to butter mixture. Sift flour with salt and pepper, add to mixture. Put dough in cookie press. Press out on ungreased cookie sheet in desired shapes. Bake at 350 degrees for 12 minutes. When cool, dust with confectioners' sugar.

Yield: 300 daisies

Kack Hodges
Washington

Raspberry Cheese Mold

1	pound white Vermont cheddar cheese, grated
1	cup pecans, chopped
1	cup mayonnaise
1	small onion, grated
1/8	teaspoon cayenne pepper
1	(12-ounce) jar seedless raspberry preserves

Combine all ingredients except preserves. Grease a ring mold with mayonnaise and press mixture into mold. Refrigerate. When ready to serve, run a knife around inner and outer circle of mold and turn over on serving plate. Fill middle of ring with raspberry preserves and serve with crackers.

For a variation, add crumbled bacon and/or chopped scallions.

Jeff Rumley
Washington

Feta and Sun-Dried Tomato Torta

1/2	cup unsalted butter, cut into pieces
3/4	pound feta cheese, crumbled
1	(8-ounce) package cream cheese
2	garlic cloves, minced
1	shallot, minced
2 to 4	tablespoons dry vermouth (optional)
	ground white pepper
1	cup pesto
1/2	cup pine nuts, toasted
1	(8-ounce) package sun-dried tomatoes, softened in water and minced

Combine butter, cheeses, garlic, shallots and vermouth in food processor or mixing bowl and blend until smooth. Season with white pepper. Oil a paté terrine, straight-sided mold, or bowl (I use an old whipped topping container) and line with plastic. Layer ingredients beginning with feta cheese mixture, pesto, pine nuts and tomatoes. Repeat. End with feta cheese mixture. Fold plastic wrap over the top and press gently to compact. Refrigerate at least one hour until firm. Invert onto a serving plate and remove plastic. Garnish with fresh basil and toasted pine nuts. Serve with crackers or bagel chips.

Emily Mayne
Washington

Pesto is an uncooked sauce made with fresh basil, garlic, pine nuts, Parmesan cheese and olive oil. Make your own fresh pesto or purchase as a dried package mix, or pre-mixed in the deli section of a fine grocery store.

Can be prepared up to 5 days in advance and refrigerated, or frozen up to 3 months.

Praline Cheese Torte

1	(8-ounce) package cream cheese, softened
1	garlic clove, minced
1	tablespoon grated onion
4	tablespoons butter
1/4	cup dark brown sugar
1	teaspoon Worcestershire sauce
1/2	teaspoon prepared mustard
1	cup pecans, chopped fine

Blend cream cheese, garlic and onion. Shape into a 6x1-inch disk and refrigerate. Melt butter and stir in remaining ingredients. Pour praline sauce over chilled cheese, cover and refrigerate. Serve at room temperature with crackers.

Lydie Jennings
Washington

Mock Liver Paté

1	(8-ounce) package cream cheese
1	(2 1/4-ounce) can deviled ham
1/2	pound Braunschweiger sausage
3	tablespoons grated onion
1/2	teaspoon Worcestershire sauce
2	tablespoons mayonnaise

Blend all ingredients until mixture is light and fluffy. Chill. Serve with sliced baguette or melba toast.

Hank Van Dorp
Washington

A famous French chef, Auguste Escoffier, developed "Melba Toast" for an Australian opera diva, Dame Nellie Melba. Escoffier must have really been enchanted by Dame Nellie because he also created the dessert, Peach Melba, which has the delicious raspberry Melba sauce.

Lindsay's Chicken Spread

2	(8-ounce) packages cream cheese, softened
1/3	cup salad dressing
1	teaspoon minced onion
1	tablespoon celery flakes
1	teaspoon Worcestershire sauce
3	chicken breasts, skinned, boiled and chopped
1/3	cup chopped fresh parsley
1/2	cup slivered almonds

Mix together cream cheese and salad dressing. Add onion, celery flakes, Worcestershire and chicken. Mix well. Chill overnight or until firm. Shape into a ball. Roll in parsley/almond mixture. Serve with crackers or bread sticks.

Beth Sloan
Washington

A favorite of my daughter, Lindsay Sloan Thorp

"I Can't Believe It's Tuna" Ball

1	(6-ounce) can white albacore tuna, packed in water
1	(8-ounce) package cream cheese
1	tablespoon lemon juice
2	teaspoons finely chopped onion
2	teaspoons horseradish
1/2	cup chopped pecans
1/2	cup finely chopped celery

Rinse and drain tuna thoroughly. Mix tuna and lemon juice, allowing the tuna to absorb the lemon juice thoroughly. Blend tuna, cream cheese, onion and horseradish. Shape into a ball and roll in pecans mixed with celery. Serve with crackers.

Lydie Jennings
Washington

Smoked Oyster Mold

1	envelope unflavored gelatin
1/4	cup dry white wine
4	ounces of cream cheese (half of 8-ounce block)
1/2	cup mayonnaise
1	(3 1/2-ounce) can smoked oysters, drained and minced
1	tablespoon minced fresh parsley
1	teaspoon Worcestershire sauce
1/4	teaspoon garlic powder
	dash of Tabasco

From a Florida friend who entertains beautifully and often!

Soften gelatin in wine. Combine cream cheese and mayonnaise in small saucepan over low heat. Stir constantly, just heating until smooth and melted. Stir in oysters and rest of ingredients. Spoon into 2 cup mold. Cover with wax paper and chill at least 2 to 3 hours before serving. Garnish with parsley. Serve with crackers.

Kaye Mayer
Washington

Shrimp Mousse

2	pounds cooked, peeled and deveined shrimp
1	can tomato soup, undiluted
6	ounces cream cheese
1	envelope plain gelatin
1/2	cup cold water
1/4	cup each, diced:
	green pepper, onion (or to taste), fresh parsley and celery
1/2	cup mayonnaise

A time-tested recipe that anchors a table of party treats.

Heat soup and cream cheese together. Dissolve gelatin in water and add to soup and cream cheese mixture. Cool. Prepare vegetables. Cut shrimp into large pieces. Mix everything together. Mold and chill. One recipe makes one large fish mold.

Mary Catherine Williams
Washington

Cajun Crabmeat Mold

2	(8-ounce) packages cream cheese, softened
2	tablespoons sour cream
1/2	teaspoon salt
1/2	teaspoon paprika
1/2	teaspoon cayenne pepper
1/4	teaspoon garlic powder
1/4	teaspoon ground thyme
1	cup cooked crabmeat
1/4	cup finely chopped green pepper
	chili pepper (optional)

Try this recipe when you are asked to bring an appetizer. This dish is a "crowd-pleaser" and travels well.

Beat all ingredients except crabmeat and green pepper in a 2 1/2-quart bowl on medium speed until well blended, about 1 minute. Stir in crabmeat and green pepper. Line a deep 1 1/2-pint bowl with plastic wrap; press mixture in bowl. Cover and refrigerate until firm, about 3 hours. Unmold on serving plate; remove plastic wrap. Garnish with chili peppers if desired. Serve with rye crackers.

Carmen Alen Potter
Aurora

Seafood for Chafing Dish

1 1/2	sticks butter
12	tablespoons all-purpose flour
4	cups milk (part can be half-and-half)
1	teaspoon or more onion flakes
2	small cans mushrooms (can use some of juice to thin sauce if needed)
	salt and pepper to taste
1	cup or more of grated sharp cheese
1/4	cup Parmesan cheese
1/2	teaspoon seafood seasoning (or to taste)
	Tabasco sauce to taste
1 1/2	pounds crabmeat
1 1/2	pounds shrimp, chopped
	vermouth or white wine, to taste

Melt butter, stirring in 1 tablespoon of flour at a time; making a paste. Add milk or half-and-half and stir, continuing to heat. Add all of remaining ingredients except seafood. Fold in the seafood once the cheeses have melted. You can use any combination of seafood (flaked white cooked fish or whatever amount of seafood you wish). Add wine to taste. Serve hot in chafing dish with patty shells, toast points or round toasted bread.

Yield: 3 quarts

Mary Catherine Williams
Washington

Oysters in Bleu Cheese

12	raw oysters, with shells
1/2	cup bleu cheese, crumbled
6	slices bacon, cooked and crumbled
	Tabasco sauce
1/2	cup crushed buttery, round crackers
1/3	cup butter, melted

Place one raw oyster in each shell. Sprinkle with cracker crumbs and drizzle with butter. Divide bleu cheese and bacon among oysters and top. Place 1 to 2 drops Tabasco on top of each. Run under broiler until bubbly.

Julie Hoell
Washington

My Raleigh Buddy's BBQ Shrimp

5	pounds shrimp (in shell)
1	quart apple cider vinegar
2	regular beers (not light)
1/4 to 1/2	cup salt
1/4	cup combined red pepper flakes and black pepper
3	tablespoons celery seed

Place all ingredients in a pot. Simmer 20 to 30 minutes until shrimp reaches desired doneness. Chill. Better served next day.

Beth Collier
Washington

Pickled Oysters

1/2	gallon oysters
	apple cider vinegar
2	tablespoons whole allspice
2	tablespoons blade mace
3	pods red pepper
	salt to taste

Cover oysters with water in a pot. Place over fire and bring to boil. Cook oysters until they start to curl. Dip oysters from pot liquor and put in bowl. Cover with vinegar and let stand a few minutes. Add pot liquor to equal the amount of vinegar. Add spices. Drain before serving. Serve very cold.

Yield: 8 servings

In memory of Frances Morgan Roberson
Submitted by her daughter, Robin Potts
Washington

On recipes of Frances Roberson:

W.R. "Bill" Roberson Jr.: "Before every family gathering, Frances would cook for about two weeks ... She cooked enough soup to float the church. I know because I delivered it...We would take New Yorkers to the airport with Zoph Potts on the piano and Edmund Harding singing in the back of a pick-up 'I'd rather wash, wash, wash, in Washington than to bathe in ancient Rome...' after a week-end junket for WITN with Frances' pickled oysters and shrimp salad. The guests thought they were in heaven."

Henderson House Crab Toast

1	pound fresh crabmeat
1/2	stick butter
1	large package processed cheese loaf
2	tablespoons horseradish
	dash of Worcestershire sauce
	juice of one lemon
2	packages English muffins

Sauté crabmeat in butter. Add cheese and cook slowly until it is melted. Add other ingredients and stir well. Place a generous amount on English muffin halves and toast. Cut English muffins into quarters.

Nancy B. Furlough
Washington

Shrimp with Vodka Dipping Sauce

2	cups mayonnaise
1/4	cup sour cream
3/4	cup bottled red chili sauce
1/4	teaspoon Tabasco sauce
4	teaspoons A-1 sauce
2	tablespoons finely chopped green onions
	black pepper (dash)
1/3	cup vodka
	steamed shrimp, peeled and deveined

Whisk together all ingredients except shrimp. Refrigerate overnight to allow for seasonings to blend.

Yield: 3 1/2 cups

Judy Lewis
Washington

Pickled Shrimp

2 1/2   pounds shrimp
1/2   cup celery tops
3 1/2   teaspoons salt
1/4   cup crab boil
4   onions, sliced into thin rings
8   whole bay leaves
1 1/4   cups salad oil
3/4   cup white vinegar
1 1/2   teaspoons salt
2 1/2   tablespoons capers, with their juice
2 1/2   teaspoons celery seed
   dash of Tabasco sauce

Put shrimp, celery tops, salt, and crab boil into boiling water. Cook until just after water returns to a boil. Drain shrimp, peel and devein, if desired.

Alternate layers of cleaned shrimp and onion rings in a shallow dish. Add bay leaves.

Combine the oil, vinegar, salt, celery seeds, capers and Tabasco. Mix well and pour over the shrimp and onions.

Cover and store in refrigerator at least 24 hours.

Nancy Murray
Washington

Chutney Sausage Balls

3   pounds sausage - 2 hot, 1 mild
2   cups sour cream
1   jar Major Grey's chutney
1/4   cup sherry

Preheat oven to 350 degrees. Blend sausages together. Form into 1-inch balls and bake approximately 15 minutes. Mix sour cream, chutney and sherry together in a blender or food processor. Pour sauce over meatballs and warm. Transfer to a chafing dish and serve with toothpicks.

Anne Stuart Rumley
Washington

Cocktail Meatballs

1 1/2	pounds ground chuck or round
4	tablespoons quick oats
1	tablespoon ginger
2	eggs
1	teaspoon salt
4	tablespoons milk
1	teaspoon minced onion
2	(3-ounce) cans mushrooms, drained and minced

Mix beef with oats, ginger, eggs, salt, milk, onion and mushrooms. Form mixture into 1 inch balls. Bake at 350 degrees for 15 minutes or until done.

Sauce

1 1/2	cups sour cream
1	teaspoon salt
1/4	teaspoon pepper
3	teaspoons horseradish (or to taste)

Heat sauce ingredients in a small saucepan (DO NOT BOIL). Place all in a chafing dish.

Barbara Ann Smith
Washington

Ducks Durango

Duck breasts (large duck)
Bacon

Durango Sauce

Worcestershire sauce
soy sauce
Texas Pete, or other hot sauce
garlic powder
salt and pepper
olive oil

Each February, I put on a "game supper" for hunting friends I have enjoyed during the season. Typical dishes are bear, rattlesnake, rabbit, turtle, alligator, dove, quail, venison, rock stew, and, of course, ducks and geese. The all-time favorite is this appetizer, which is served hot from the grill.

Several days prior to serving, cut large duck breasts into finger-size strips, approximately 3/4 inch wide and the length of the breast. Liberally cover with salt, pepper and garlic powder. Set aside. Combine all other ingredients, with 2 parts olive oil to I part Worcestershire and soy sauce, each. Salt, pepper and garlic to taste. Cut raw bacon strips in half. Wrap bacon around the strips of duck, securing with a toothpick. Place in flat glass 9x13-inch casserole dish. Pour Durango sauce over strips, covering completely. Marinate for 2 days, turning each day. Bank charcoal and allow to glow red hot. Spread coals. Place strips on grill, turning with long handled tongs. (They will flame up and that's good!) Cook approximately 2 to 3 minutes per side. Do not overcook. Remove to plate and serve immediately.

Wayland J. Sermons, Jr.
Washington

Tempting Tenderloin

1	5 to 6 pound beef tenderloin
6	tablespoons yellow mustard
6	tablespoons Worcestershire sauce
3 to 4	liberal shakes Tabasco sauce
	onion powder
	garlic salt
	black pepper
1	stick butter, melted

Rub the tenderloin with the onion powder, garlic salt and black pepper, making sure to turn it over so as to cover both sides. Mix the mustard and Worcestershire sauce together and cover the entire tenderloin with this mixture.

Shake hot sauce randomly over the top of the beef and pour butter over this. The beef may be prepared early in the day, but remove from the refrigerator at least an hour and to an hour and a half before you plan to begin cooking. Turn oven to broil setting and place the tenderloin on the top rack under the broiler for ten minutes. This sears the beef and should create a crust on the top. Watch closely when broiling and remove sooner if it appears to have formed a crust.

Remove pan from oven, lower the temperature to 425 degrees and place tenderloin on center rack. Use an instant-read thermometer; 120 degrees is rare; 125 to 130 degrees is medium-rare; and 135 to 140 degrees is medium. The baking process generally translates into 5 to 6 minutes per pound, but it is safer to use a thermometer. Remove beef from oven and allow to sit for 15 to 20 minutes before carving.

To grill, prepare tenderloin as you would to bake it but sear the meat under the broiler 10 minutes on one side, then turn over and sear 10 minutes on the other side. Remove from oven and place on a hot grill, using an instant-read thermometer to reach preferred doneness. When you remove the tenderloin from the grill, the temperature will rise 5 degrees; allow for this in your cooking time. Allow beef to rest 15 to 20 minutes before carving. Just a reminder: Always insert the thermometer into the thickest part of the beef. Slice, serve with rolls and horseradish sauce.

Horseradish Sauce

2	cups sour cream
1 1/2	tablespoons cream-style prepared horseradish
1	tablespoon Worcestershire sauce
	salt to taste

My favorite recipe which I brought to Washington from Winston-Salem. Serves a crowd for a cocktail buffet. Easy!

I have used this same marinade, minus the stick of butter, on different cuts of steak, always with great success.

Sarah Sloan
Washington

Pizzazz

1/2	pound kielbasa sausage
1	pound chicken livers
1	box frozen Brussels sprouts
1	can whole water chestnuts, drained

Optional additions:
cocktail onions, meatballs, or button mushrooms

Cook kielbasa according to package directions and cut into bite-size pieces. Bake chicken livers at 350 degrees for 35 minutes. Cook Brussels sprouts for 8 minutes. Combine all ingredients and keep warm while making the following sauce.

Sauce

1	cup mayonnaise
1/3	cup horseradish
2	teaspoons lemon juice
1/2	teaspoon salt
2	teaspoons dry mustard

Combine all ingredients. Warm in double boiler, stirring constantly. Sauce will separate if boiled. Place "Pizzazz" in chafing dish and serve with toothpicks.

Hank Van Dorp
Washington

Bourbon Pork Tenderloin

1/4	cup soy sauce
1/4	cup bourbon
2	tablespoons brown sugar
2 1/2 to 3	pounds pork tenderloin

Preheat oven to 325 degrees. Mix ingredients and marinate pork several hours, turning occasionally. Bake I hour, basting several times with marinade. Boil leftover marinade and pour over tenderloin that has been sliced thin. Serve on bite-sized yeast rolls.

Archie Jennings
Washington

Sweet-N-Sassy Wings

5   pounds chicken wings and drummettes
1   (2-pound) bag brown sugar
    chopped garlic
1   (15-ounce) bottle Worcestershire sauce

Spread wings and drummettes in two 9x13-inch pans. Liberally cover chicken with brown sugar, sprinkle with garlic and pour Worcestershire sauce over sugar and garlic. Use enough Worcestershire sauce so sugar somewhat dissolves. Bake at 350 degrees for 20 to 30 minutes, stirring occasionally. Drain on foil. Serve warm, room temperature, or cold; any way, they are great!

Joan Campbell
Washington

Coffee Punch

2   cups water, boiling
2   cups sugar
3   tablespoons instant coffee

Bring these ingredients to a boil and cool. Add:

1   gallon skim milk
1/4   gallon chocolate ice cream
1/4 to 1/2 gallon vanilla ice cream

Stir together and serve. Makes one large punch bowl, serving a good-sized group.

Jan De Hoog
Terra Ceia

Summer Daiquiri

1   (6-ounce) can frozen lemonade concentrate
6   ounces dark rum
1/3 to 1/2 cup half and half
            ice

Add all to blender and blend on high until smooth.

Yield: 1 pitcher

Julie Hoell
Washington

Terra Ceia

In the 1920's some Dutch families were encouraged to move from the Netherlands to Beaufort County to develop truck farms.

They soon discovered that the soil was better suited for raising tulips. They founded the community that is now known as Terra Ceia, which means 'Heavenly Soil.' Flower farming continues to be a way of life in this unique community.

Brenda's Naval Officer's Lemonade

This is a recipe from my sister Brenda. Her husband is a Captain in the Navy, and they do lots of entertaining. You have to adjust the sugar to taste—be careful, this drink will slip up on you!

1   bottle Chardonnay
8   lemons, squeezed
2   cups sugar

Mix all ingredients and pour over a pitcher of crushed ice. You may need additional sugar. Cut up a lemon and add to the pitcher for garnish.

Yield: 1 pitcher

Nancy B. Furlough
Washington

Champagne Punch

If it's a warm day and a convivial crowd, it might be wise to be prepared for everyone to require refills, so count on 8 ounces per guest. Do not serve to minors. I served this at a bridal shower and caught the mother of the bride with some cohorts tipping the punch bowl and scraping to get the last drops, I made another batch and they actually licked the bowl clean!! It is strong and wonderful ... maybe it should be served on the groom's table, uh?

1 1/2   cups powdered sugar
1/2   cup curacao or orange flavored liquor
1/2   cup cognac
1/2   cup maraschino cherry juice
1   quart pineapple sherbet
3   bottles champagne
1   orange, sliced
1   lemon, sliced

Chill the punch bowl. Mix sugar and curacao thoroughly in a pitcher. Stir in cognac and cherry juice. Pour into punch bowl; gently place block of sherbet in center. Slowly add champagne and garnish with fruit slices. (Fruit will be prettier if small notches are cut in outer rim of rind to resemble flower petals.) Do not stir the punch after champagne is added.

Yield: About 25 (punch cup) servings; triple or quadruple recipe for a reception for 40 to 50.

Pamela Gunnin Burkart
Washington

French 75s

3   whole lemons, freshly squeezed
1   cup freshly squeezed orange juice
4   teaspoons sugar
1/3   cup brandy
3   dashes bitters
     crushed ice
     champagne

Mix lemon juice, orange juice, sugar, brandy and bitters. Fill glasses with crushed ice and equally divide syrup among four glasses and top with champagne.

Yield: 4 servings

Nancy Murray
Washington

Named for the Napoleonic cannons, these are sure-fire blasters!!!! Be sure to have all drinkers sign a waiver holding you blameless for any actions after consumption of these wicked wonders.

Mr. Allen's Old Crow Punch

1   fifth Old Crow
1   (6-ounce) can frozen lemonade concentrate
1   (6-ounce) can frozen orange juice concentrate
1/3   cup cherry juice
1   quart soda

Blend all ingredients. (Make an ice ring: Add 2 inches of water to a bundt pan and freeze. Add cherries, holly, orange or lemon slices and fill to the top and freeze again. Remove form by running hot water on exterior of pan.) Put in punch bowl with above mixture.

Herbert Hoell
Washington

In the 1950s, "Big Band Weekends" were held in a local tobacco warehouse. Three well-known orchestras would play for dances on three consecutive nights. These dances were held in the summer without air conditioning. A hot time was had by all!

Rum-Cranberry Punch

2	cups light rum
1/2	cup sugar
1	(12-ounce) can frozen orange juice concentrate, thawed and undiluted
1	(32-ounce) bottle cranberry juice, chilled
1	(28-ounce) bottle ginger ale, chilled
	orange slices
	strawberries

Combine rum, sugar, orange juice, and cranberry juice. Just before serving, add ginger ale and ice cubes. Garnish with orange slices and strawberries.

Note: Substitute pineapple juice for rum, if desired.

Yield: About 2 1/2 quarts

Barbara Francisco
Washington

"EEII's Little Korners of the World" has been part of the Belhaven landscape for nearly thirty years. "EEII" is Effie Raye Goff, artist, teacher, and a life-time promoter of artists. She is equally famous for her "Twilight Hours" receptions featuring lemonade or apple cider served with cinnamon crisps. For smaller groups, she served a delicious "Christmas in July" eggnog with strawberries floating on top.

Pain Killers

1	fifth dark rum
1	(46-ounce) can unsweetened pineapple juice
1	(15-ounce) can cream of coconut, shake well
1	(6-ounce) can orange juice concentrate

Pour all ingredients in a gallon milk jug and shake. Freeze approximately 24 hours. Cut off top of milk jug. Spoon mixture into glass and garnish with nutmeg.

Archie Jennings
Washington

Jeffrey Jakub

Fruits of Our Labor

watercolor

Soups, Salads & Sandwiches

Summer Melon Soup

1   large very, very, very ripe honey dew melon, peeled and diced
        chopped basil and mint (couple of tablespoons)
3   limes, zested
3   fresh squeezed limes (same that you zested)
1 to 2 heaping tablespoons yogurt
1/2   cucumber, peeled, seeded and chopped

Place all ingredients in blender and purée. Chill in refrigerator for two or more hours. Serve.

Marcus Rios
former Washington resident

Shipping was our means of obtaining fresh fruit in the early 1900s. Oranges, coconuts, pineapples, and bananas were brought from the West Indies. The main item, however, was molasses by the barrel.

Gazpacho

8   tomatoes, peeled, or 1 (15-ounce) can whole tomatoes
1   quart water
1/2   loaf French bread or 5 to 6 slices American bread, soaked in water
1   onion
3   cloves garlic
        juice of 1 lemon
1/2   cup wine vinegar
1/2   teaspoon Tabasco sauce
        pepper and salt to taste
1/2   cucumber, peeled and cubed
3   green peppers, chopped
1   cup almonds

Blend all ingredients except half a cucumber, one green pepper, and 1/2 cup almonds, filling the blender only three-quarters full each time to ensure proper blending. It makes no difference in what order you blend your vegetables; in other words, you can blend all your tomatoes at one go or combine them with whatever else might fit to make your blender three-quarters full. Empty the blender loads into your soup tureen, and stir to make sure all ingredients are evenly mixed.

Add the remaining half cucumber, the green pepper, and the almonds, coarsely chopped. Refrigerate. If you've had no time to refrigerate, you can add 3 or 4 ice cubes directly to the soup tureen.

Yield: 4 to 5 servings

In memory of Frances Morgan Roberson
Submitted by her daughter, Robin R. Potts
Washington

Black Bean and Pasta Soup

1 1/2	tablespoons olive oil
2	celery stalks, chopped
1	small white or yellow onion, chopped
2	cloves of garlic, chopped,
6	cups vegetable broth (For a low-sodium version, use less broth and dilute with water to 6 cups.)
1	cup dried pastina (elbow macaroni, farfallini, or other tiny shapes)
1	bay leaf
1	(14-ounce) can whole black beans, drained
1	(14-ounce) can chopped tomatoes
	salt and pepper, to taste
	grated Parmesan cheese, to serve (optional)

Heat the olive oil in a Dutch oven or other large saucepan. Gently fry celery, onion and garlic for 2 to 3 minutes. Add the vegetable broth and stir occasionally until warm. Add the pastina and bay leaf. Stir in the black beans and tomatoes. Season with salt and pepper. Bring the soup to a boil, then reduce heat and simmer for 15 minutes. Serve with grated Parmesan cheese, if desired.

Yield: 4 to 6 servings

Karen Brothers
Washington

Chicken Gumbo

5	cups cooked chicken, cubed
2	cans tomatoes (jalapeño seasoned or other)
1	can chicken broth
1	package frozen okra, cut-up
3/4	cup rice, cooked
	season to taste - parsley, Worcestershire sauce, garlic powder, red pepper, salt and pepper

This is a favorite of my grandchildren.

Cook chicken with enough water to cover in a large pot. Remove chicken from pot, cool, skin and de-bone; cut into pieces. Retain stock and to it add chicken, canned broth, tomatoes, okra and seasonings. Bring to a boil. Simmer for 1 hour. Add cooked rice for last 15 minutes.

Lynn Sermons
Washington

Chicken Vegetable Soup

1	whole chicken
1	large onion, sliced
3	celery stalks, sliced
2	(28-ounce) cans diced tomatoes with juice
3	carrots, sliced
1/2	cup rice
3 to 4	(14-ounce) cans chicken broth, depending on thickness you like
1	(8-ounce) package frozen white corn
1	(16-ounce) package frozen butter beans
1	bay leaf
	bouquet garni

Parsley, thyme and bay leaf, tied together or placed in a cheese cloth bag, comprise the classic bouquet garni. Remove the herbs before serving.

In a large pot, place chicken and cover with salted water. Simmer, covered until chicken is tender. Remove chicken. Leave stock in pot. Chill stock to skim fat from top. Skin and bone chicken, cut into pieces and reserve.

Add sliced onion to chicken stock, along with chopped celery and leaves. Add 2 cans tomatoes with juice, bay leaf, and bouquet garni. Cook about one hour. Add sliced carrots, and butter beans and cook until tender, about 30 minutes. Add 1/2 cup rice and cut up chicken. Add canned chicken broth as needed. Cook about 15 minutes. Add frozen corn and cook 5 minutes. Add salt and pepper to taste.

Lily G. Grimes
Washington

Homemade Vegetable Soup

Julia never measured; this soup "makes a gracious plenty."

1	shoulder or chuck roast, about two pounds
1	(28-ounce) can tomatoes
2	teaspoons each, sugar, salt and pepper
1	large onion, cut up
1	rib celery, cut up
2	potatoes, cut up
1	carrot, cut up
1/2	package each of corn and butter beans, frozen
1	small can cut string beans
1	small can green peas
	small amount of spaghetti, cut into one-inch lengths, or macaroni

Partially freeze shoulder or chuck roast and cut into about one-inch pieces. Combine with tomatoes, large onion, sugar, salt and pepper. Cook in soup pot until meat is tender, about two hours. Add potatoes, celery and carrot. Cook about 15 minutes. Add corn, butter beans, string beans, green peas, and pasta and bring to a boil. Cook until pasta is done, approximately 10 minutes.

In memory of Julia Mitchell
Submitted by Betty Mitchell Gray
Washington

Greek Lemon Soup

May be served hot or cold. My family likes this soup best when it is served cold. If reheated, do so very carefully, stirring constantly over low heat. To serve, garnish with lemon slices.

6	cups chicken broth
1/3	cup rice, uncooked
1	teaspoon salt
3	eggs
1/4	cup lemon juice
2	lemons, thinly sliced for garnish

In saucepan, bring broth to a boil over high heat. Pour in rice. Reduce heat to low and simmer partially covered for about 15 minutes or until grains are just tender. In deep, narrow bowl, beat eggs well. Add 1/2 cup boiling broth to lemon juice. Now beating or whisking constantly, add the lemon-broth mixture to the beaten eggs very slowly. Next, add the lemon-egg mixture to the chicken broth in pan on stove. Whisk, then stir over low heat about 3 minutes, or until mixture thickens to coat spoon lightly. DO NOT LET SOUP BOIL - it will curdle.

Yield: 6 servings

Louise Lane
Washington

Erwtensoep (Dutch Pea Soup)

1	package green split peas, soaked overnight in 3 quarts cold water
2	pounds smoked ham hocks or a ham bone with some meat on it
	salt and pepper to taste
1	onion, cut up
3	celery stalks, cut up
2	carrots, sliced (optional)

Drain peas, cook with ham bone or ham hocks in plenty of water for 1 1/2 to 2 hours. Take meat from bones and return meat to the cook pot. Add salt, pepper, and cut-up vegetables. At this point, cut up fresh or smoked sausage may be added. Simmer for another hour, stirring often to make certain soup is not sticking to bottom of pot.

This is a winter soup. It tastes much better the day after it is cooked. Make certain it is served hot.

Yield: 6 servings

Gerda Tigchelaar
Terra Ceia

In Holland when ice is on the Dutch canals, vendors sell the hot soup to the skaters.

Spring Pea Soup

12 to 16	ounces peas, frozen or fresh
3	cups whole milk
1	clove garlic
1 to 2	mint leaves
	salt to taste

Add all ingredients together in soup pot. Heat to a boil. Turn off heat. Pour into blender. Purée for 3 minutes. Garnish with mint.

Yield: 4 to 6 servings

Marcus Rios
former Washington resident

Meaty Potato Soup

3 to 5   pounds potatoes
1   pound kielbasa sausage, cut into 1/4-inch slices
2   onions, one chopped coarse and one chopped in eighths
1   tablespoon chicken bouillon granules
       salt and pepper to taste

Peel potatoes, cut in equal quarter sizes or larger. Place in Dutch oven, cover with water and cook until halfway fork tender. Drain potatoes, place them back into Dutch oven, cover with fresh water, add the onions and cook until potatoes are fork tender. Add salt and pepper to taste. Take one cup of the pot liquor and mix it with the chicken bouillon and return to the soup. Add kielbasa sausage and simmer 1/2 hour, stirring occasionally.

Doug Davis
Washington

Mushroom and Potato Chowder

Sausage can be added for the meat lover.

1/2   cup chopped onion
1/2   cup butter, divided
2   tablespoons all-purpose flour
1   teaspoon salt
1/2   teaspoon pepper
3   cups water
1   pound mushrooms, sliced
1   cup chopped celery
1   cup diced, peeled potatoes
1/2   cup chopped carrots
1   cup heavy cream
1/4   cup grated Parmesan cheese

In a large kettle, sauté onion in only 1/4 cup butter until tender. Add flour, salt and pepper; stir to make a smooth paste. Gradually add water, stirring constantly. Bring to a boil; cook and stir for 1 minute. Add vegetables. Reduce heat; cover and simmer for 30 minutes or until vegetables are tender. Add cream, rest of butter, and sprinkle Parmesan cheese on top.

Yield: 4 to 6 servings

Karen Glass
former Belhaven resident

Fish Chowder

1/4	cup diced salt pork
1	cup sliced celery
1/2	cup chopped onion
2	cans cream of potato soup
2	soup cans milk
1	pound fillet of whitefish, cut in 1 inch pieces
1	cup sliced cooked carrots
1	(8-ounce) can whole kernel corn, drained
1/8	teaspoon pepper
1	medium bay leaf

In saucepan, brown salt pork. Remove pork. In drippings, cook celery and onion until tender. Add pork, soup, milk, whitefish, cooked carrots, corn, pepper, bay leaf. Stir and bring to a boil. Reduce heat. Simmer 10 minutes or until fish is done. Stir often. Note: If chowder is too thick, add more milk.

Yield: 8 1/2 cups

Mary C. Hull
Washington

Take your boat out in the Pamlico River and catch dinner. Find a spot across from Chocowinity to cast your line. Chocowinity means "fish-from-many-waters."

Mary French's Shrimp Chowder

3 to 4	large onions, chopped
1	stick butter, melted
5	medium white potatoes, cubed
2	pounds shrimp
3	cups half and half or cream
1	cup cubed processed cheese loaf
	salt and pepper, to taste

Sauté onions in butter until limp. Set aside. In a large saucepan or Dutch oven, cover potatoes with water and cook until done, 20 to 30 minutes. Set aside. Boil shrimp about 3 minutes, or until pink. Drain and cut into small bite-sized pieces. Next, heat cream over medium heat. Add cheese and stir continuously. DO NOT BOIL. Add shrimp, onions and potatoes with their remaining juices. Thin to preferred consistency with cream. Add seasonings.

Yield: 15 servings

Beth Collier
Washington

Manhattan Clam Chowder

1/4	pound salt pork, finely chopped
2 1/2	cups diced potatoes
1 or more	carrots, chopped
3/4	cup finely chopped onion
1/2	cup finely chopped celery
	green pepper, if desired
1	quart clams, chopped
1 1/2	quart clam liquor and water
1	clove finely chopped garlic
1	bay leaf
1 1/2	teaspoon thyme
1	teaspoon salt (optional)
	pepper
2 1/2	cups stewed tomatoes

Sauté onion, garlic and salt pork. Cook vegetables in very little water until tender. Open clams, conserving any liquor. Cut in chunks and drain. Strain liquor, throw away any residue on bottom. Let stand 10 minutes. Repeat at least twice more. Add clams to liquor and cook gently 10 to 15 minutes. Combine all ingredients and simmer. Mash some or all potatoes if you want a thicker soup.

Linda Seale
Washington

Pamlico River Crab Stew

This is a delicious way to enjoy summer's bounty! I spent many summer days as a child catching blue crabs from the pier. My grandmother would fix this stew in the evening, a real treat for everyone, and it still is.

12	large Jimmy Crabs, cleaned and halved
12	ears of Silver Queen corn, cut from the cob
6	new potatoes, peeled and quartered
1	large onion, diced
1	tablespoon of butter
	salt and pepper to taste

Sauté onion until tender. Add potatoes and cover with water. Add salt and pepper to taste. Boil for 20 minutes. Add corn, return to a boil. Add crabs, and simmer for 10 minutes.

Cover table with newspapers. Serve stew in large bowls. Provide crab knives so diners can crack the crab shells and extract the meat. Provide plenty of napkins.

Yield: 4 servings

Linda Boyer
Washington

New England Clam Chowder

1/2	pound bacon, diced
1	cup chopped leeks
1	cup chopped yellow onion
1/2	cup chopped celery
1	carrot, peeled and diced
3	bay leaves
1	tablespoon chopped fresh thyme, (or 1 teaspoon dried)
1/2	cup all-purpose flour
1	pound new or red potatoes, peeled and diced
4	cups clam juice
2	cups half and half
8	cans (6 1/2-ounce) minced clams (save juice; this will yield 4 cups)
2	tablespoons finely chopped parsley
	salt and pepper, to taste

In large heavy pot, render bacon over medium heat until crispy. Stir in leeks, onions, celery and carrot. Sauté until vegetables start to wilt. Season with salt and pepper. Add bay leaves and thyme. Stir in flour and cook for 3 minutes. Add potatoes and clam juice. Bring to a boil and reduce heat to simmer. Simmer until potatoes are fork tender, about 10 minutes. Add half and half and bring back to a simmer. Add clams and simmer 3 minutes. Stir in parsley and season again with salt and pepper.

Note: After adding flour and clam juice, if mixture becomes too thick, add a bit of water. Also, after rendering bacon you can pour off some of the bacon grease, saving some for flavor.

Yield: 6 to 8 servings

Margaret Dorn
Washington

Shrimp-Chickpea Soup Maxwell

Crumbled, sautéed, spicy Italian sausage can be substituted for the shrimp.

1 1/2 cups chickpeas, soaked overnight in cold water
2   tablespoons olive oil
2   onions, chopped
2   cloves garlic, chopped
1   potato, peeled and sliced
1/2   teaspoon black pepper
5   cups chicken or vegetable stock
1/4   cup butter
6   cups washed spinach, cut in strips
1 1/2 pounds shrimp, peeled, deveined, and cut in half
1/4   cup almonds, toasted, chopped

Drain chickpeas and rinse well. Put in a saucepan, cover with cold water, bring to a boil and simmer, covered, for about 1 hour. Drain and set aside. Heat olive oil, add onions and cook until translucent. Add garlic, stock, pepper, potato slices, and add half of the chickpeas. Simmer until chickpeas and potatoes are falling apart. Cool and purée in blender. Return to saucepan and adjust seasonings. Bring to a simmer and add the rest of the chickpeas, spinach, shrimp, and 1/4 cup of toasted, chopped almonds. Cook until shrimp turns pink.

Yield: 8 to 10 servings

Joan Conlon
Washington

Catfish Gumbo

1   pound catfish fillets
1   cup chopped celery
1/2   cup chopped green pepper
1/2   cup chopped onion
2   medium garlic cloves, finely chopped
2   tablespoons vegetable oil
2   cups chicken broth
1   (14-ounce) can tomatoes
1   (10-ounce) package okra
1/4   teaspoon red pepper, crushed
1   teaspoon gumbo filé (season to taste)
1 1/2 cups hot cooked rice

Cut catfish into 1 inch pieces. Cook celery, green pepper, onion and garlic in vegetable oil in Dutch oven until tender. Add broth, tomatoes, okra, red peppers, gumbo filé and seasoning. Cover and simmer 20 minutes. Place fish on vegetables. Cover and simmer 15 minutes longer or until fish flakes easily when tested. Serve with hot rice.

Yield: 6 servings

Roy Tucker
Chocowinity

Rockefeller Soup

2	quarts chicken stock
2	medium onions, diced
2	cups chopped spinach (pack down in cup to measure)
1/2	teaspoon nutmeg or mace
1	bay leaf
1 or 2	drops Tabasco sauce
4	tablespoons butter
1/2	cup all-purpose flour
1	cup milk
1	cup cream
1	pint fresh oysters, reserve liquid
1/2	cup sherry

Bring stock to boil. Skim if needed. Add diced onions to stock and reduce heat to simmer. Add spinach, nutmeg, bay leaf and Tabasco. Cover and simmer until onions are translucent. In small pan, stir butter and flour together over low heat to make a pale roux, stirring often. Gradually whisk in milk, and add cream last. Add this mixture gradually to stock mixture, stirring well. Add salt and pepper to taste. Finally, add oysters and simmer until oysters curl slightly. Taste and correct seasoning if needed. Stir in the sherry. Serve hot.

Yield: 8 one cup servings

Louise Lane
Washington

Toast strips are good with this soup. You may garnish with a bit of chopped spinach. This soup can be reheated if done very slowly while stirring.

Seafood Bisque

1	pound medium-size fresh shrimp, scallops, and/or crabmeat
2	tablespoons butter
1/4	cup butter
1	cup sliced fresh mushrooms
1/4	cup chopped green onions
1	garlic clove, minced
3	tablespoons all-purpose flour
1	(10.5-ounce) can condensed chicken broth, undiluted
1/2	cup dry white wine
1/2	cup whipping cream
1	tablespoon chopped fresh parsley

Peel shrimp; sauté seafood lightly in 2 tablespoons of butter. Melt 1/4 cup butter in a large heavy saucepan. Sauté mushrooms, green onions, and garlic about 5 minutes or until tender. Add flour, stirring until smooth; cook over medium heat, stirring constantly, 1 minute. Gradually add chicken broth; cook, stirring constantly, until thickened and bubbly.

Add seafood; reduce heat, and simmer, stirring often, 3 minutes. Stir in wine, whipping cream, and parsley; cook, stirring often, until thoroughly heated.

Yield: 4 cups

Cathy Whichard
Washington

Brunswick Stew

1	(3-pound) chicken, cut in pieces
2	quarts chicken broth (can dilute by adding water)
	salt and pepper
1/4	cup diced uncooked bacon
1	cup chopped onion
2	cups tomatoes, peeled and drained or 1 (19-ounce) can tomatoes
2	cups peeled and diced raw potatoes
2	cups fresh lima beans or 1 (10-ounce) package frozen
2	cups fresh corn (about 8 ears)
1	tablespoon Worcestershire sauce
2	tablespoons butter

Put chicken, salt and pepper into kettle. Simmer until chicken is tender, skimming often to remove fat and foam. Remove chicken from broth and continue to boil to reduce broth slightly. When cool, remove chicken from bones and return to kettle. Add bacon, onion, tomatoes, potatoes and lima beans. Cook until vegetables are tender, approximately 20 minutes. Skim to remove fat and stir to prevent sticking. Add corn and cook 10 minutes longer. When done, stew should be quite thick. Add butter and Worcestershire sauce.

Yield: 8 to 10 servings

Sadie Fowle
Washington

Venison Chili

6	tablespoons of butter
6	medium onions, sliced
3	pounds ground venison
2	(28-ounce) cans of tomatoes
1	(6-ounce) can tomato paste
1 1/2	cups beer
2	teaspoons of salt
1 1/2	teaspoons of hot sauce
3	tablespoons chili powder

Melt butter in a large saucepan and add onions. Cook until transparent, add venison and cook until browned. Add tomatoes, tomato paste, beer, salt, hot sauce and chili powder. Reduce heat and simmer for 45 minutes.

Yield: 4 to 6 servings

This is good served over rice or spaghetti.

Lewis Sloan
Washington

Black Bean Vegetable Chili

A low-fat recipe that is so good no one will notice!

1	large onion, chopped coarsely
1	tablespoon olive oil
1	(28-ounce) can whole tomatoes, undrained and chopped
2/3	cup picante sauce (choose heat to your liking)
1 1/2	teaspoons ground cumin
1	teaspoon salt
1/2	teaspoon basil
1	(16-ounce) can black beans, rinsed and drained
1	(8-ounce) can pork and beans, optional
1	green bell pepper, cut into 3/4-inch pieces
1	red pepper, cut into 3/4-inch pieces
1	large yellow squash or zucchini, cut into 1/2-inch chunks (2 cups)
1/4	cup white wine, optional

Optional toppings: hot cooked rice, sour cream, shredded cheese.

Cook onions in olive oil until soft. Add tomatoes, picante sauce and seasonings. Cover and simmer 5 minutes. Stir in beans, peppers and squash and cook 5 minutes more. Cover and simmer until vegetables are tender, about 15 minutes. Ladle into bowls, top as desired and serve with additional picante sauce.

Yield: About 8 one cup servings

Irene Forbes
Washington

Broccoli with Sun-Dried Tomatoes and Pine Nuts

1	head broccoli, about 1 pound
3	tablespoons balsamic vinegar
1	small garlic clove, minced
5	tablespoons extra virgin olive oil
	salt and pepper
2	sun-dried tomatoes, thinly sliced
2	tablespoons pine nuts, toasted
	champagne vinegar (this can be left out if unavailable)

Cut the broccoli into florets about 1 1/2 inches long. Peel broccoli stems. In a small bowl, whisk together the balsamic vinegar, garlic, oil, 1/2 teaspoon of salt and a few pinches of pepper.

Bring a medium-sized pot of water to a boil. Add 1/2 teaspoon salt. Drop in the broccoli stems and cook for about 3 minutes, adding the florets at the last minute. The broccoli should be bright green and slightly crisp. Drain and rinse with cold water. Toss the broccoli with the sun-dried tomatoes, pine nuts and vinaigrette. Add salt and pepper to taste and a splash of champagne vinegar.

Yield: 4 to 6 servings

Kara and Mike Crawford
Washington

Garden Fresh Cucumber Salad

1/4	cup vinegar
1	tablespoon lemon juice
1/2	teaspoon celery seeds
2	tablespoons sugar
3/4	teaspoon salt
1/8	teaspoon pepper
2	onions, chopped
3	cups sliced, peeled cucumbers (2 medium)

I've used this recipe a lot. I like to prepare food ahead of time and this works well.

Combine all ingredients and pour over cucumbers. Chill.

Yield: 3 cups.

Helen Myers
Pantego

Karen's Italian Salad

1	head lettuce, torn
2 to 3	cans Mandarin oranges, drained
1	can ripe black olives, pitted
1	cup shredded mozzarella, provolone or Monterey Jack
1/2	cup sunflower seeds
	croutons
	Parmesan cheese

This is a recipe my neighbor in Phoenix, Arizona, shared with me!

Toss all together and add dressing;

1/2	cup red wine vinegar
1/4	cup extra light olive oil
1	tablespoon Italian seasonings or Italian dressing mix

Yield: 6 to 8 servings

Lucy Cheshire
Washington

Jerusalem Artichoke Salad

This delightful salad is made from Beaufort County's native artichoke, not the Globe or French artichoke. It grows wild and looks like a small sunflower. If grown in the garden, be sure to control it or the tubers will take over. The tubers can be eaten as a vegetable, pickled or used as a substitute for water chestnuts.

4	raw artichokes, washed well and peeled
1/4	cup fresh lemon juice
1/4	cup fresh chives, chopped
1	cup lettuce, chopped or shredded
	French dressing

Slice artichokes into very thin rounds. Spread rounds in a shallow bowl. Pour lemon juice over them and let marinate 15 to 20 minutes. Put chives and lettuce into 4 bowls for serving. Drain artichokes and evenly distribute among the bowls. Pour desired amount of dressing over each salad and serve.

Yield: 4 servings

Louise Lane
Washington

New York Salad

1 1/2 bunches fresh, raw spinach
1   quart strawberries, washed and sliced
1   red onion, thinly sliced

Dressing

1/2   cup mayonnaise
2   tablespoons sugar
1   tablespoon lemon juice
1 1/2 teaspoons poppy seed

Mix spinach, strawberries and onion together. Prepare dressing and toss just before serving.

Yield: 6 to 8 servings

Karen Glass
former resident of Belhaven

Marinated Coleslaw

1   large head of cabbage, shredded
1   green pepper, thinly sliced
1   large onion, thinly sliced

Place in layers in the above order in a large bowl.

Pour over all:
1   cup sugar (do not stir)

Combine:
3 /4   cup oil
1   cup vinegar
1   teaspoon dry mustard
1   teaspoon celery seed
1   teaspoon salt

Bring to the boiling point. Pour over cabbage while hot. Do not stir. Refrigerate overnight.

Yield: 10 servings

Sadie Fowle
Washington

Sauerkraut Salad

This is Mark's recipe. It's like a cole slaw without all that shredding. Good with Brunswick stew and great with Rueben sandwiches.

1 1/2   cups sugar
1/3   cup water
2/3   cup cider vinegar
1/3   cup vegetable oil
2   (15-ounce) cans sauerkraut, drained and washed
1   cup chopped onion
1   cup chopped celery
1   green pepper, chopped
1   can water chestnuts, sliced
1   large jar pimiento, chopped

Dissolve sugar in water. Add oil and vinegar. Heat. Combine remaining ingredients. Pour vinegar mixture over all. Mix well. Chill. Keeps indefinitely refrigerated.

Yield: 8 to 10 servings

Nancy Collis
Washington

Tomato and Feta Cheese Salad

2 to 3 tomatoes, diced
1   red onion, sliced
1   tablespoon fresh basil
1   (4-ounce) package feta cheese, crumbled
2   tablespoons olive oil
2   tablespoons red wine vinegar
1   tablespoon mustard

Mix well for a good summer salad.

Yield: 4 to 6 servings

Lou Hollowell
Aurora

Grapefruit Salad

5   grapefruit
4   packages lemon gelatin
2   cups boiling water

Dressing

3   tablespoons all-purpose flour
1/3   cup sugar
3   egg yolks, well-beaten
3   lemons, juiced
1   cup pineapple juice
10   marshmallows
1   cup slivered almonds
1/2   pint whipping cream, whipped

This recipe is over 50 years old. It is festive and a great compliment to poultry and ham. Mom and I often use it during the holidays as a change of pace with our turkey dinners. Although the dressing contains cream, the overall effect of the salad is light and refreshing.

Cut grapefruit in half the long way. Scoop out the pulp and juice, making sure both the pulp and juice, as well as the grapefruit halves, are free of pith and membrane. Set aside pulp and juice and save halves. Dissolve lemon gelatin in the boiling water, add grapefruit juice and pulp. Stir. Fill grapefruit halves and chill. To make the dressing, mix the flour and sugar, then add the yolks, lemon juice and pineapple juice. Cook in double boiler until thick. Remove from heat; stir in marshmallows and almonds until marshmallows have dissolved. Whip the cream and gently stir into the lemon mixture. Chill.

To serve, cut each grapefruit shell in half, place each wedge on a lettuce leaf, and dollop generously with dressing. Pass remaining dressing at table. Note: I usually double the dressing recipe because it is so popular. Any left over can be used with fresh fruit.

Yield: 20 servings - 4 per grapefruit

Connie Howard
Washington

Colonial Inn Frozen Fruit Salad

1	(8-ounce) package cream cheese
4	tablespoons mayonnaise
2	(8-ounce) cartons frozen non-dairy whipped topping
1	(9-ounce) can pineapple, drained
1	large jar sliced maraschino cherries, drained (save juice)
2	big handfuls of miniature marshmallows

Beat to soften cream cheese and mix with mayonnaise. Add pineapple and cherries. Add non-dairy topping and stir in marshmallows. Finally, add enough cherry juice to make mixture pink. Put into 9x13-inch pan and freeze.

Yield: 12 servings

Lee M. Vann
Washington

Tomato Aspic with Shrimp

1	(3-ounce) package lemon gelatin
2	cups tomato juice
1	lemon, juiced
2	tablespoons vinegar
1	tablespoon Worcestershire sauce
1/2	teaspoon salt
1/3	cup finely chopped onion
1/3	cup finely chopped green bell pepper
1/3	cup finely chopped celery
1	teaspoon plain gelatin
1/2 to 1 pound shrimp, cooked	

Dissolve gelatin in 1 cup hot tomato juice. Add other ingredients and pour into a greased mold or glass dish. Chill until congealed. (Tomato-vegetable juice may be used.)

Yield: 6 to 8 servings

Mary Paulson
Chocowinity

Shrimp Salad

2   pounds shrimp, cooked until just done and sliced lengthwise
2   cups celery, chopped diagonally
2   tablespoons lemon juice
1/4   teaspoon seasoning salt
2   cups mayonnaise
1/2   cup minced onion

Mix mayonnaise and shrimp together. Lightly fold in remaining ingredients. Serve over sliced tomatoes.

Yield: 6 servings

In memory of Frances Morgan Roberson
Submitted by her daughter, Robin Potts
Washington

Creamy Tomato Aspic Ring

2   tablespoons unflavored gelatin
1/2   cup cold water
2   (8-ounce) cans tomato sauce
2   tablespoons lemon juice
1   cup sour cream
1/2   cup Rhine wine
1/2   teaspoon salt
1   tablespoon instant minced onion
3   tablespoons cold water
2   tablespoons minced parsley
1   cup thinly sliced celery

Soften gelatin in 1/2 cup cold water. Heat tomato sauce to boiling. Add gelatin. Stir until dissolved. Add lemon juice, sour cream, Rhine wine and salt. Chill until slightly thickened. Meanwhile, combine onion and 3 tablespoons of cold water. Let stand until water is absorbed. Fold into thickened gelatin with parsley and celery. Spoon into 5 cup ring mold. Chill until set. Unmold. Garnish with stuffed olives and watercress or parsley.

Yield: 6 to 8 servings

Terry Knott
Washington

Sunshine Salad

1	small package lemon gelatin
1	(14 1/2-ounce) can crushed pineapple, juice and fruit separated
1	tablespoon vinegar
	pinch of salt
1	cup cold water
1/2	cup mayonnaise
1	cup shredded carrots
1	cup shredded cheddar cheese
1	cup shredded celery
1/2	cup nuts (in small pieces)

Heat pineapple juice and dissolve gelatin. Add vinegar, salt, water. Cool. Add mayonnaise, pineapple, carrots, cheese, celery and nuts. Chill.

Yield: 8 servings

Frances Larkin
Washington

Shrimp Pasta Salad

"Al dente" means "to the tooth", an Italian term describing pasta cooked until it offers a slight resistance when you bite a strand.

2	pounds shrimp, boiled until just done
1	(16-ounce) package shell macaroni, cooked al dente
2	cups diced tomatoes
1	(2 1/2-ounce or more) can black olives, sliced
6	ounces feta cheese, crumbled
	oregano, salt and pepper to taste
	red wine vinegar and olive oil to taste

Toss all ingredients together. May be served at room temperature or refrigerated.

Dr. Tom Speros
Washington

Flying Farmer Chicken Salad

5	cups cooked chicken, cut in chunks
2	tablespoons salad oil
2	tablespoons orange Juice
2	tablespoons vinegar
3	cups cooked white or brown rice
1 1/2	cups seedless green grapes
1 1/2	cups chopped celery
1	(13 1/2-ounce) can pineapple tid-bits
1	(11-ounce) can Mandarin oranges, drained
1	cup toasted slivered almonds
1/2	cup mayonnaise

Combine chicken, oil, orange juice, and vinegar. Let above stand while preparing other ingredients. Refrigerate overnight. Gently toss together all ingredients.

Yield: 12 servings

Shirley Padgett
Washington

This recipe goes back to my teaching days in Pennsylvania. It was always a big hit when we teachers had a pot-luck supper. It can be made ahead and kept for several days. It is beautiful served in a canteloupe on lettuce, with clusters of grapes decorating the plate.

Lila Duke's Cranberry Salad

1	quart fresh cranberries, rinsed
1	(20-ounce) can crushed pineapple, undrained
1	orange
1	cup pecans, chopped
2	packages cherry or raspberry gelatin
3/4	cup sugar

Cut whole orange into quarters. Cut out white membrane. Grind cranberries and orange together. Sprinkle sugar over mixture. Add pineapple with juice and nuts. Pour 2 1/2 cups of boiling water over gelatin. Stir in cranberry mixture and chill.

Yield: 10 servings

Jean Duke Trueblood
Washington

This was my mother's recipe that many Washingtonians enjoyed through the years. Her name was Lila Roper Duke (Mrs. J. Frank Duke). My family and I still enjoy it.

Chicken Salad with Cranberry Dressing

4	cups cooked, diced chicken
1	cup chopped celery
1/2	teaspoon salt
1/2	teaspoon pepper
1/2	cup mayonnaise
1/2	cup sour cream
	salted pecans or toasted almonds
3/4	cup salad oil
1/4	cup vinegar
1	teaspoon salt
1	teaspoon sugar
1/2	teaspoon paprika
1/4	teaspoon dry mustard
	dash of pepper
1/2	cup jellied cranberry sauce

Mix first six ingredients. Divide into 4 to 6 servings. Sprinkle each serving with nuts. Make dressing by combining all remaining ingredients, except cranberry sauce, in a jar. Shake until blended. Gradually blend vinaigrette into cranberry sauce, beating until smooth. Spoon dressing over each salad.

Yield: 4 to 6 servings

Mary Paulson
Chocowinity

Hot German Potato Salad

1/2	pound bacon
5	potatoes, cooked in jackets
1	onion, chopped
1/2	teaspoon salt
1/4	teaspoon pepper
1	teaspoon sugar
1/2	cup vinegar
1	beaten egg
3	tablespoons water

Cook bacon until crisp. Crumble bacon and add to potatoes and onion. Add remaining ingredients to bacon drippings. Heat thoroughly, stirring constantly. Pour over potato mixture and mix well. Serve immediately.

Yield: 6 servings

Jane Fields
Washington

Lemon Potato Salad

6	red or white potatoes (about 3 pounds)
2	cups chopped celery
2	cups broccoli florets
1	cup thinly sliced Vidalia onion
2	carrots, sliced
2	small tomatoes, seeded and chopped
2	cups mayonnaise
2/3	cup lemon juice
3	tablespoons (or more) chopped fresh mint
1	teaspoon salt
1	teaspoon pepper

In a saucepan, cook unpeeled potatoes in water to cover until tender; drain and cool. Peel and cut into cubes. Combine with the celery, broccoli, onion, carrots and tomatoes in a large bowl. Combine the mayonnaise, lemon juice, mint, salt and pepper in a small bowl. Mix well. Add the dressing to the vegetables; toss gently to mix. Chill until serving time.

Yield: 10 servings

Betty Anne Dicken
Washington

Serve this with lemon twists and additional sprigs of mint for garnish. This is a colorful salad, and the lemon is a nice variation of the traditional potato salad.

Grilled Rosemary Potato Salad

5	tablespoons olive oil
1	tablespoon minced rosemary or 1 teaspoon dried
2	tablespoons white wine
3	tablespoons mayonnaise
1	tablespoon white wine vinegar
1	teaspoon Dijon mustard
2	medium scallions, sliced thin crosswise
3	tablespoons minced parsley
	salt and pepper
1 1/2	pounds small new potatoes, halved

Mix oil and rosemary in a small bowl; set aside. Mix next 6 ingredients plus 1/2 teaspoon salt and 1/4 teaspoon pepper in a small glass bowl; cover and refrigerate. (This can be done the day before.)

Put the potatoes and 2 teaspoons salt in a large saucepan; cover with water and boil about 12 minutes until just tender; drain.

Heat the grill. Drizzle rosemary oil over potatoes; toss well. Put potatoes on the grill, cut side down, and cook, turning frequently, until tender and brown in spots, about 8 minutes.

To serve, transfer potatoes to a serving bowl; toss with the mayonnaise mixture. Serve warm or at room temperature.

Yield: 4 servings

Wanda Johnson
Washington

Moonbeam Salad

2	teaspoons olive oil, divided
1	teaspoon dried oregano
1	garlic clove, minced
1/4	cup cider vinegar
2	(16-ounce) cans cannellini beans, rinsed and drained
1 1/2	cups diced fresh plum tomatoes
1/2	cup chopped sweet onion
1/2	cup crumbled blue cheese (2-ounce package)
1/3	cup chopped fresh parsley
1/2	teaspoon salt
1/2	teaspoon pepper

Heat 1 teaspoon oil in non-stick skillet over a medium heat. Add oregano and garlic. Sauté 30 seconds. Add vinegar and remove from heat. Combine vinegar mixture and beans in a bowl. Cover and chill 2 hours.

Add teaspoon oil, tomatoes and the next 5 ingredients to bean mixture. Toss well and serve.

Yield: 10 servings

Ethel Schramm
Chocowinity

Mediterranean Pasta

4	cups chopped tomatoes (vine-ripened or plum)
2	tablespoons chopped fresh basil
3	tablespoons chopped black olives
1	tablespoon olive oil
1	tablespoon red wine vinegar
1/4	teaspoon salt
1/8	teaspoon crushed red pepper
1	garlic clove, minced
4	cups angel hair pasta (or thin spaghetti), cooked
1/4	cup crumbled feta cheese

A great, easy, light summer dish shared by a healthy young friend.

Combine first 8 ingredients in a bowl. Stir and let stand 10 minutes. Serve at room temperature stirred into pasta. Sprinkle with feta cheese.

Yield: 4 small servings

Jingle Robinson
Washington

Edna's Wild Rice Salad

This is good with beef or game.

2   (6-ounce) packages wild rice (may use long grain)
1   cup chopped dates (cherries or golden raisins may be used)
1/2   cup chopped green onions
1/2   cup pecans, toasted
4   Italian tomatoes, chopped or 6 sun-dried tomatoes, reconstituted and chopped
1   cup olive oil
2   tablespoons lemon juice
2   tablespoons vinegar
1   teaspoon dry mustard
1   teaspoon dried basil
2   garlic cloves, minced
1   teaspoon black pepper
1/3   cup chopped parsley

Cook rice. Cool. Combine dry ingredients: dates, onions, pecans, tomatoes, rice. Combine dressing ingredients (remaining ingredients). Shake well. Pour over rice combination. Mix well and serve.

Katirie Leach
Washington

Hatteras Marlin Club Tuna Salad

Even if you don't like tuna, you owe it to yourself to try this. The Hatteras Marlin Club is famous for its food and this is excellent.

1 1/2   pounds fresh tuna, washed with dark meat removed
1   whole lemon
3/4   cup chopped celery
1/4   cup chopped onions
        salt
        pepper
1/4   cup sweet pickle relish
1/2   cup mayonnaise
1   tablespoon Dijon mustard

Put cleaned and washed tuna in water. Add juice and fruit of a whole lemon and boil for 10 minutes. Drain and cook again for additional 10 to 20 minutes. Let cool and break into large flakes. Add remaining ingredients and mix well. (Use more or less mayonnaise for desired consistency.) Chill well and serve.

Yield: 6 servings

Gray Murray
Washington

Nonne's Tuna Nicoise

1	can tuna in water, drained
	capers
	black olives
	mustard
	olive oil
	green beans, fresh, cooked
	potatoes, cooked and cubed
	onion, chopped
	red wine vinegar
	salt and fresh ground pepper

Low fat and tasty.

Rub salad bowl with garlic clove. Mix together and chill. Use the amounts you like of each.

Yield: 4 servings

Catherine Partrick
Washington

Sarah's Pimiento Cheese

1 1/2	pounds block medium cheddar cheese
1	(7-ounce) jar sliced pimientos
5	heaping tablespoons mayonnaise
2	tablespoons apple cider vinegar
2	tablespoons sugar
2	teaspoons Worcestershire sauce
	several shakes of black pepper
	several shakes of cayenne pepper

Process cheese in food processor, with grating blade. Combine cheese with pimientos and juice, sugar, vinegar, Worcestershire sauce, mayonnaise, black and red pepper and mix by hand until well blended.

This is best made a day ahead of time. Two variations: add 2 tablespoons of horseradish to above recipe or add 1/4 cup of grated Vidalia onion to above recipe. This is good served on crackers, as a sandwich spread or to stuff celery hearts.

Sarah Sloan
Washington

Miss Carver's Chili for Chili Dogs

The story goes that a little boy went to Miss Carver's with 10 cents in his pocket. He asked Miss Carver what he could buy. She gave him a hot dog bun with chili and no hot dog – thus came the "chili dog!"

2	pounds lean ground round steak
1 1/2	teaspoons onion salt
1	tablespoon chili powder
1	(16-ounce) can tomato puree

Brown meat. Add other ingredients. If mixture is too thick, rinse the tomato puree can out with a little water and add to mixture. Simmer on low heat.

Elsie Lois Carver
former Washington resident

Open-Faced Luncheon Sandwiches

Dressing

3/4	cup mayonnaise
1/4	cup chili sauce
2	tablespoons chopped green onions
1	(9-ounce) can pineapple tidbits
1/2	cup whipping cream, whipped stiff and folded into 4 previous ingredients

Assemble in this order:

8	slices of French bread, buttered and toasted
	lettuce
	tomato
	chicken or turkey, sliced
	sliced egg
	dressing

Serve with knife and fork.

Yield: 8 servings

Anne Stuart Rumley
Washington

Willie Watson Sandwich

Place a slice of branola, rye or whole wheat bread on a plate. Cover with crisp lettuce, slice of turkey, slice of ham, one green pepper ring, slice of cheddar cheese, slice of roast beef, 2 purple onion rings, and 2 slices of crisp bacon.

To prepare sauce, thin mayonnaise with boiling water, enough to give it a consistency that will dribble and season with garlic or garlic salt.

In memory of Mary Wilson
Washington

Italian Picnic Loaf - Southern Style

1	10-inch round soft white bread (may use Hawaiian Bread)
8	slices Smithfield-type ham, thinly sliced
8	slices pastrami, thinly sliced
8	slices smoked turkey breast, thinly sliced
8	slices roast beef, thinly sliced
8	slices provolone cheese, thinly sliced
8	slices Havarti cheese, thinly sliced (or may use Swiss, if desired)
2	(6-ounce) jars marinated artichoke hearts (may use less, if desired)
1	(2-ounce) jar pimientos, drained well
2	tablespoons olive oil

The early 1900s found many young couples taking a picnic lunch out to Cow Head Springs for an afternoon outing at the spring.

Carefully cut bread in half to make 2 flat rounds. Remove inside of each half, leaving a shell with 1 inch border. Brush each half with olive oil. Drain artichokes and reserve marinade. Place bottom shell on plate. Put layer of 4 slices of turkey on bottom, then 4 slices of pastrami. Scatter artichoke pieces (about 6) over this, adding 1 or 2 tablespoons marinade. Continue layering in any way you wish, being certain to space the cheeses apart. Use drained pimiento in a single layer through the middle, ending with a meat on top. Use marinade and artichokes throughout loaf. Place top shell over this. Press down firmly. Put another dinner plate on top of the sandwich and cover tightly all over with plastic wrap. Now weight this down with 2 or 3 one-pound cans and let rest in refrigerator at least 8 hours or overnight.

When ready to serve, remove cans and wrapping and cut into 8 wedges. This is very hearty so only pickled cucumbers, sliced tomatoes or a small green salad, plus fruit for dessert is needed for a full meal.

Yield: 8 to 10 servings

Louise Lane
Washington

Oyster Sub

Edgar's Pool Room in downtown Washington served the very best roast pork combination sandwiches. Sadly, Edgar Woolard's recipe remains secret.

1	loaf French or Italian bread
	garlic butter
6 to 7	slices bacon
1	pint fresh oysters
1	fresh tomato
	mayonnaise
	horseradish (creamed)

Split bread lengthwise. Take out center, leaving 1/4 inch on sides and bottom. Brush inside of bread with garlic butter. Make garlic butter by melting butter and sautéing garlic. Do not let butter brown, or garlic will be bitter.

Fry 6 or 7 slices of bacon crisp and then crumble. Save 1/2 of this grease and fry oysters over medium heat until outer edges begin to curl. Use 1/2 of oyster juice to fry.

Take oysters out with slotted spoon. Slice enough tomatoes (1/4 inch thick) to cover length of bread. Place tomatoes in the skillet where the bacon and oysters were cooked and heat until soft. Place oysters in bread cavity, layer bacon and tomato. Salt and pepper, if you wish. Place two pieces of bread together, roll in foil, place on a rack in 400 degree oven for approximately 20 to 25 minutes.

While loaf bakes, mix mayonnaise and horseradish to the taste you like. Remove loaf from oven and slice in 2 to 3-inch thick servings. Use sauce to your taste. If you have a sauce you prefer, use it.

Yield: 4 to 6 servings

Vance Smith
Washington

Quick Hot Crab "Open Sandwiches"

1/2	stick margarine or butter
8	ounces crabmeat
8	ounces processed cheese loaf, or sharper cheese, shredded
1/2	teaspoon garlic powder
	dry mustard (just a dash)
1/2	teaspoon seasoning salt
	Worcestershire sauce
2 1/2	tablespoons mayonnaise
	paprika

Easy and quick to prepare!

Slowly heat all together. Heap on half English muffin. Sprinkle with paprika and toast at 350 degrees or until bubbly.

Yield: 6 to 8 servings

Frances Hulbert
Washington

Dinglewood Pharmacy's "Scrambled" Hot Dog

12	hot dogs
12	hot dog buns
3	(16-ounce) cans chili with no beans
1	(6-ounce) jar prepared mustard
1	(12-ounce) jar sweet salad cubes
1 1/2	cups onions, chopped
2	cups cheddar cheese, shredded
2	cups oyster crackers

Cook hot dogs (boil or zap). Place hot dogs in the buns and put on individual plates (2 per plate). Cut each into 6 pieces and top with chili and next 4 ingredients. Sprinkle with crackers. Serve with a fork and spoon.

Yield: 6 servings

Gray Murray
Washington

Stroganoff Steak Sandwich

2/3	cup beer
1/3	cup cooking oil
1	teaspoon salt
1/4	teaspoon garlic powder
1/4	teaspoon pepper
2	pounds flank steak, about I inch thick
2	tablespoons butter
1/2	teaspoon paprika
4	cups sliced onion
1	cup sour cream, warmed
1/2	teaspoon prepared horseradish
12	slices French bread, toasted

A zesty beer marinade gives the flank steak an unforgettable flavor.

In shallow dish, combine beer, oil, salt, garlic powder, and pepper. Place flank steak in marinade. Cover. Marinate overnight in refrigerator or several hours at room temperature. Drain. Broil flank steak about 3 inches from heat for 5 to 7 minutes on each side for medium rare. In saucepan, melt butter. Blend in paprika and a dash of salt. Add slices of onion; cook until tender but not brown. Thinly slice meat on the diagonal across the grain. For each serving, arrange meat slices over 2 slices of French bread. Top with onions. Combine sour cream and horseradish, spoon onto each sandwich. Sprinkle with paprika, if desired.

Yield: 6 to 8 servings

Sue Nicholson
Bath

Bettie Bonner Bradshaw

The Flower Vendor

watercolor

Breads

Sourdough Steel-Cut Oats Bread

2	cups boiling water
2	cups steel-cut oats
1/4	cup honey
2	cups whole wheat flour
1 1/2	cups sourdough starter
1	package dry yeast
1/2	cup warm water
1/2	cup melted butter
1/2	cup pure maple syrup
2	teaspoons salt (optional)
4 1/2 to 5	cups graham flour or whole wheat flour

Pour boiling water over steel-cut oats and let stand until lukewarm. Then stir in honey, 2 cups of whole wheat flour, and the starter. Blend thoroughly and let stand for several hours — or if weather is quite cool, let mixture stand overnight. This is called the "sponge."

When the sponge is ready, dissolve the yeast in warm water and add to the sponge with rest of the ingredients. . Blend well and turn out onto a lightly floured surface. Knead for about 8 to 10 minutes, adding more flour as necessary to make a firm, unsticky dough. It should be smooth and elastic.

Place in buttered bowl, turn to coat all sides, cover, and let rise in warm place for about I hour. Turn out onto floured surface and knead again for about 2 to 3 minutes. Divide into 3 portions, shape into loaves, and place in 3 buttered 9x5-inch loaf pans. Cover and let rise in warm place until almost double size.

Bake at 350 degrees for 45 to 50 minutes. Cool on wire racks.

Yield: 3 loaves

Bea Simmons
Washington

Very good – and good for you. Look for steel-cut oats in the health food section of your grocery store.

From the Washington Daily News - May, 1992

"Alice Jennette Lee is recognized as a stalwart figure in the Pantego community. In 1949, she purchased a grocery store which evolved into one of the area's favorite restaurants, complete with home-made booths and tables." Mrs. Lee's reputation for home-cooking and generosity spread, earning her the name of "Mama Lee." A specialty of hers was cheese biscuits.

Bran Bread

4	cups all bran cereal
3 1/2	cups sour milk
1/2	cup solid vegetable shortening
1	cup sugar
1/4	cup molasses
1/4	cup honey
4	eggs
1	cup applesauce
2	teaspoons soda
4	teaspoons baking powder
2	teaspoons salt
4	cups all-purpose flour

To sour sweet milk, add 1 tablespoon white vinegar or lemon juice to each one cup of milk. Let stand for a few minutes.

Soak bran cereal in sour milk. Cream shortening and sugar; add molasses and honey. Beat eggs and add to shortening and sugar mixture. Add applesauce, sour milk and bran cereal. Sift soda, baking powder and salt with flour and blend with mixture.

Pour into 3 greased 9x5-inch loaf pans. Bake at 375 degrees for 1 hour. Be sure to check and not overbake.

Yield: 3 loaves

Sylvia Evans
Washington

Helen Sommerkamp
Aurora

Pumpkin Banana Bread

1 1/2 cups sugar
1/2   cup shortening
2   eggs
1   cup (2 large) mashed ripe bananas
1 3/4 cup canned solid pack pumpkin
1   teaspoon vanilla extract
1 3/4 cups all-purpose flour
2   teaspoons baking powder
1   teaspoon baking soda
1/2   teaspoon salt
1/2   cup chopped pecans or walnuts
       halved nuts for garnish

In large bowl, cream sugar and shortening. Beat in eggs, bananas, pumpkin and vanilla; mix well. In medium bowl, combine flour, baking powder, baking soda, salt and nuts. Add dry ingredients to pumpkin mixture, mix well. Spoon batter into greased and floured 9x5-inch loaf pan. Top with nuts if desired.

Bake in preheated 350 degree oven 55 to 65 minutes or until wooden pick inserted in center comes out clean. Cool 10 minutes, remove from pan. Serve warm, or cool on wire rack.

Yield: 1 loaf

Johanna and Leonard Huber
Washington

Nancy Murray
Washington

Most breads freeze well for later use.

Zucchini Bread

This is a dark and moist bread, and very tasty.

3	eggs
1	cup sugar
1/3	cup molasses
1/3	cup oil
1	tablespoon vanilla
2	cups shredded zucchini, packed
1 2/3	cups graham cracker crumbs
1 1/2	cups all-purpose flour
1	tablespoon plus 1 teaspoon cinnamon
2	teaspoons baking soda
1/2	teaspoon baking powder
1	cup chopped nuts

Mix eggs, sugar, molasses, oil, vanilla and zucchini together. Then mix in all remaining ingredients.

Put into 2 greased and floured 9x5-inch loaf pans and bake at 350 degrees for 50 to 60 minutes.

Yield: 2 loaves

Ann Van Staalduinen
Terra Ceia

Carrot Bread

Very rich and moist - these freeze nicely.

3	cups all-purpose flour
2	cups sugar
2	cups shredded carrots
1 1/2	cups vegetable oil
1	(8-ounce) can crushed pineapple
3	eggs
3	tablespoons cinnamon
1	teaspoon baking soda
1	teaspoon salt

Preheat oven to 325 degrees. Grease and flour 2 9x5-inch loaf pans or 6 mini loaf pans. Combine all ingredients in a large mixing bowl. Pour batter into loaf pans. Bake 45 to 60 minutes, until tester inserted in center comes out clean.

Yield: 2 loaves or 6 mini loaves.

Lind Graves
Washington

Hawaiian Banana Nut Bread

3	cups all-purpose flour
3/4	teaspoon salt
1	teaspoon baking soda
2	cups sugar
1	teaspoon ground cinnamon
1	cup chopped pecans or walnuts
3	eggs, beaten
1	cup vegetable oil
2	cups mashed ripe bananas
1	(8-ounce) can crushed pineapple, drained
2	teaspoons vanilla extract

Combine first five ingredients; stir in pecans. Combine remaining ingredients; add to flour mixture, stirring just until dry ingredients are moistened. Spoon batter Into two greased and floured 8 1/2 x 4 1/2 x 3-inch loafpans. Bake at 350 degrees for one hour and 10 minutes, or until a wooden pick inserted in center comes out clean. Cool in pans 10 minutes; remove from pans and let cool on wire racks.

Yield: 2 loaves

Louise Bright
Chocowinity

Barbara Ann Smith
Washington

Southern Spoon Bread

3	cups milk
1	cup white corn meal
1	tablespoon melted butter
1	teaspoon sugar
1	teaspoon salt
3	egg yolks, beaten
3	eggs whites, stiffly beaten

Preheat oven to 350 degrees. Grease a 1 1/2-quart casserole (round) with butter. Scald milk in top of double boiler: Add corn meal gradually. Cook 5 minutes, stirring until smooth. Cool slightly. Add butter, sugar and salt. Add beaten egg yolks; fold in egg whites. Pour into casserole dish. Bake 45 minutes. Serve immediately.

Lib Ross
Lucy Cheshire
Washington

A big part of Beaufort County's culinary heritage:

Lace-edge Cornbread

1	cup white cornmeal
1 1/2	cups buttermilk
1/2	teaspoon soda
1/2	teaspoon salt
1	egg, beaten

Slowly add egg and buttermilk to the sifted dry ingredients. Beat until very smooth. Have iron frypan hot and filled with about 2 tablespoons oil. Drop cakes by tablespoon into hot oil. Do not crowd; allow to spread. When brown on one side, turn and brown other. As batter tends to thicken, add more milk. Drain on paper towels.

Batter can also be made using only meal, water and egg.

Remove any bits of batter from pan that may get too brown.

Stuffed Picnic Bread

1   package active dry yeast
1   cup warm water (110 degrees)
3   cups all-purpose flour
1   egg
1   tablespoon butter
1   tablespoon sugar
1   teaspoon salt
1   cup chopped ham
1   cup shredded mozzarella cheese
1   (4-ounce) jar diced pimiento peppers, drained
1/2   cup black olives, drained and chopped

In a small mixing bowl, dissolve yeast in warm water. Let stand until creamy, about 10 minutes. In a large mixing bowl, combine the yeast mixture with the flour, egg, butter, sugar and salt; mix well. When the dough has pulled together, turn it out onto a lightly floured surface and knead until smooth, about 8 minutes. Lightly oil a large mixing bowl, place the dough in the bowl and turn to coat with oil. Cover with a damp cloth and let rise in a warm place until doubled in volume, about 1 hour. Preheat oven to 400 degrees. Combine the ham, cheese, pimiento and olives in a medium mixing bowl; set aside. Deflate the dough and turn it out onto a lightly floured surface. Roll or pat the dough into a 10x14-inch rectangle. Make parallel cuts 3/4-inch wide and 2-inches long on the two long edges of the rectangle. Evenly spread the filling mixture over the center of the rectangle. Fold the short ends of the rectangle over the filling. Starting from one of these ends alternately stretch strips from the two sides across the filling so that the strips overlap diagonally. Transfer the loaf to a lightly greased baking sheet, cover with a damp cloth and let rise until doubled in volume, about 40 minutes. Bake at 400 degrees for 20 to 30 minutes or until golden brown.

Yield: 1 loaf

Carmen Alen Potter
Aurora

Hush Puppies

2	cups white cornmeal
2	cups all-purpose flour
3	tablespoons baking powder
2	teaspoons salt
1	teaspoon pepper
1	medium onion, finely chopped
3	scant cups milk

Sift dry ingredients into a mixing bowl and add chopped onion. Stir in the milk until ingredients are well mixed. Drop by teaspoons in hot deep fat. Cook until puffed and golden brown, about 3 or 4 minutes.

Yield: 6 to 7 dozen

Sue Nicholson
Bath

Keep more than the dogs satisfied with a batch of "hush puppies," a Southern specialty once used to keep begging dogs quiet while dinner was being prepared. Husbands and children enjoy these deep-fried treats, too.

The Interim Pastor's Hush Puppy Recipe

2	cups Aunt Jemima's pancake mix
1	cup V-8 juice
1	small onion, minced
1/2	teaspoon Tabasco sauce

Mix together. Drop by spoonful into heated cooking oil and cook until lightly browned on the outside.

F. Harry Daniel
Washington

Fresh Herb Foccacia

This is a modification of the hearty foccacia of Italy. The crust is crisp on the outside while it is chewy and moist on the inside. Your kitchen will be wonderfully perfumed with the fragrance of Italy: sharp cheese, fresh herbs, garlic, and olive oil. Serve with a green salad.

1	package active dry yeast
1	cup plus 2 tablespoons warm water
	pinch of sugar
1	cup regular boiled grits, cold
2	tablespoons olive oil, plus 1 1/2 tablespoons olive oil for top of dough
4 to 4 1/2	cups bread flour
1 1/2	teaspoons salt

Place the yeast, 2 tablespoons water, and the sugar in a large mixing bowl. Let sit until foamy, about 10 minutes.

Put the grits, the remaining 1 cup water, and the oil in a mixer and run until smooth. Pour the grits mixture into the proofed yeast. Add 4 cups of the flour and salt and beat hard. Transfer the dough to a work surface and knead vigorously adding more flour if necessary to prevent sticking, 8 to 10 minutes. Put the dough in a bowl, cover, and let rise in a warm place until doubled, about 1 hour.

Divide dough in half. Put on floured surface, flatten, and make two 12 -inch circles. Put each on greased and cornmeal-covered pizza pan, and brush top surface of dough with about 1 1/2 tablespoons olive oil. Cover and let rise until looks puffy but not quite doubled, about 20 minutes.

Preheat oven to 450 degrees.

Topping

Cooked grits in small quantities give breads a fine, crisp crust and strong, elastic texture to the crumb. The high-starch and low-protein content of corn complements the wheat flour well.

4	tablespoons olive oil
1	(4-ounce) package feta cheese, crumbled
1 1/2 to 2	cups chopped fresh herbs, such as basil, thyme, parsley, oregano, sage and rosemary
2	large cloves garlic, chopped
10	ounces shredded mozzarella
1	cup freshly grated Parmesan cheese

Mix the feta cheese, 4 tablespoons of olive oil, the herbs, and garlic. Sprinkle this cheese mixture over the top of the dough. Bake about 20 minutes. Sprinkle with the mozzarella and Parmesan, return to the oven, and finish baking about 10 more minutes. It should be beautifully golden with a terrific aroma. Cool for a few minutes on a rack, then serve hot.

Yield: two 12-inch focacce

Sue Mansfield
Washington

Refrigerator Rolls

1	cup mashed potatoes (2 medium size)
2/3	cup butter
1/4	cup honey
1	teaspoon salt (optional)
2	eggs
1	package dry yeast
1/2	cup warm water
1	cup milk, scalded and cooled to lukewarm
6 to 7	cups whole wheat flour
	melted butter

Combine mashed potatoes, butter, honey, salt, and eggs and cream them well. Dissolve yeast in the lukewarm water, add to the milk, and then add to potato mixture. Add enough flour to make a stiff dough. Turn out onto lightly floured board and knead for about 8 minutes. Put the dough in a large, greased bowl, cover, and let rise to double size in a warm place (about 1 to 2 hours). Knead down lightly, rub top with melted butter, cover tightly, and place in refrigerator until ready to bake.

About 1 hour before baking time, roll dough out on a floured surface, cut in rounds using a biscuit cutter, place on greased cookie sheet. Let rise, lightly covered, in a warm area for about 45 to 60 minutes. Bake at 375 degrees for about 20 minutes or until well done.

Yield: 4 to 5 dozen

Bea Simmons
Washington

Butterhorn Rolls

1	package active dry yeast
1/3	cup warm water
1/2	cup sugar
1/2	cup shortening
2	teaspoons salt
2/3	cup milk
5 to 5 1/4	cups sifted all-purpose flour
3	slightly beaten eggs
	melted butter

Soften yeast in warm water for about 5 minutes. Combine sugar, shortening, salt and milk; scald, stirring until shortening melts and sugar dissolves; cool to luke-warm. Add 1 1/2 cups flour; beat well. Add softened yeast and eggs; beat well. Stir in remaining flour or enough to make a soft dough, 1/2 cup at a time.

Turn out on floured surface. Knead lightly until smooth and elastic, 5 to 8 minutes. Place dough in lightly greased bowl, turning once to grease surface. Cover with clean dish towel; let rise in a warm place until double, about 3 hours. Punch down. Turn out on lightly floured surface.

Divide dough into three equal pieces; round each into a ball. Cover and let rest 10 minutes. Roll each to 12-inch circle, about 1/4 inch thick. Brush with melted butter. Cut each circle in 12 wedges. To shape, grasp wedge at the corners of end opposite point and start to roll up away from you. Now flip the point toward you.

Arrange rolls, points down, on greased baking sheets and brush with melted butter. Cover and let rise in warm place until double, about 1 hour. Bake at 400 degrees for 10 minutes or until done. Bake only 7 to 8 minutes if you are going to freeze and reheat. You can use 2 packages of yeast; the first rise is 1 1/2 hour and second will be 50 minutes.

Yield: 3 dozen.

Wilma Wells
Washington

Make Ahead Yeast Rolls

2	packages dry yeast
1 1/4	cup warm water
3	large eggs, slightly beaten
1/2	cup melted butter
2	teaspoons salt
1/2	cup sugar
4 1/2 to 5	cups bread flour

Combine yeast and water; let stand 5 minutes. Beat eggs in mixer and add butter, salt, sugar, yeast mixture and 2 cups flour. Beat 2 minutes. Add rest of flour and beat until smooth. Cover and let rise 1 hour. Punch down and refrigerate 8 hours or overnight. Punch down, knead 3 or 4 times. Divide in half and shape 16 rolls from each half. Put into lightly buttered 9-inch square pans. Cover and let rise 1 1/2 hours. Bake at 375 degrees for 12 minutes or until lightly browned.

Yield: 32 rolls

Helen Myers
Pantego

My favorite quick roll recipe. I mix it on Friday, put it in pans on Saturday and bake it on Sunday after it rises while I'm in church. What a wonderful smell to come home to; this and meat loaf!

Bran Muffins

1	cup all-purpose flour
1/2	cup brown sugar
2 1/2	teaspoons baking powder
1/2	teaspoon baking soda
1/2	teaspoon salt
1 1/4	cups bran
1	cup milk
1	egg
1/4	cup canola oil
1/2	cup raisins (optional)

Preheat oven to 400 degrees. Blend the first five ingredients together in a bowl. Set aside. Stir together bran and milk and let stand five minutes. Add egg and oil; beat until blended. Add flour mixture. Add raisins. Stir until everything is well blended. Fill greased muffin tins two-thirds full. Bake 20 minutes.

Yield: 8 muffins

Phebie Mills
Chocowinity

Pumpkin Muffins

My aunt gave me this recipe many years ago. It is a delicious addition to a Thanksgiving breakfast - or any fall breakfast, for that matter.

3   cups all-purpose flour
4   teaspoons baking powder
1 1/2 teaspoons salt
1   cup sugar
1   teaspoon cinnamon
1   teaspoon nutmeg
1/2   cup butter
1   cup raisins
2   eggs
1   cup canned pumpkin
1   cup milk

Stir together dry ingredients. Cut in butter to make a coarse meal. Add raisins. Combine beaten eggs with pumpkin and milk. Add to the dry mixture, mixing only to combine. Fill greased muffin pans two-thirds full. Sprinkle 1/4 teaspoon sugar over each muffin. Bake in hot oven (400 degrees) for 18 to 20 minutes. Serve hot.

Yield: 24 muffins

Jane Fields
Washington

Oatmeal-Date Muffins

1   cup whole wheat flour
1   cup rolled oats
1   cup corn meal
1/2   teaspoon salt
4   teaspoons baking powder
1   cup chopped dates/nuts/raisins mixture
1   egg
1/4   cup melted butter
1 1/2 cups buttermilk

Preheat oven to 400 degrees. Combine dry ingredients including date/nuts and raisins. Add egg, butter and buttermilk and stir until just blended. Do not over mix. Bake 20 to 25 minutes.

Yield: 12 muffins

Frances Hulbert
Washington

Morning Glory Muffins

2 1/4   cups all-purpose flour
1 1/4   cups sugar
1   tablespoon cinnamon
1/2   teaspoon salt
2   teaspoons soda
1   cup grated carrots
1   whole Granny Smith apple, grated
1/2   cup raisins
1/2   cup broken walnuts
1   (8-ounce) can crushed pineapple, drained
1/2   cup shredded coconut
3   eggs, slightly beaten
1   teaspoon vanilla
2/3   cup vegetable oil

Sift dry ingredients together. Mix fruits and nuts in separate bowl. Mix eggs, vanilla and oil; add to fruit mix, then add dry mix to all. Add sifted ingredients to above mixture. Fill muffin tins to brim. Bake at 400 degrees for 35 to 40 minutes. Cool in pan 10 minutes before removing. Surprisingly enough, these do not have to be heated before serving.

Yield: 16 muffins

Laura Bell
Washington

This is one of my best recipes. The batter keeps well in the refrigerator 2 weeks before baking and after baking the muffins freeze well.

Ice Cream Muffins

2   cups self-rising flour
2   cups softened vanilla ice cream
1   egg, beaten
2   tablespoons cooking oil

Combine flour and softened ice cream. Add egg and oil and beat until smooth. Fill greased muffin pans 3/4 full. Bake at 325 degrees for 20 minutes.

Yield: 12 muffins

Kathryn Nunnally
Washington

Orange Blossoms

1/2	cup butter
1	cup sugar
3	eggs
1/2	cup milk
2	cups all-purpose flour
2	teaspoons baking powder
1	teaspoon vanilla

Cream butter and sugar; add eggs and beat. Sift flour and baking powder together; add alternately with milk. Add vanilla. Bake in greased mini-muffin pans at 350 degrees for 10 minutes.

Icing

1	orange, juice and grated rind
1	lemon, juice and grated rind
2	cups confectioners' sugar, sifted

Combine and stir until smooth. Dip muffins in icing as soon as they are removed from the oven. Dry on a rack. The secret is not to get too brown, just barely brown. The muffins freeze well.

Yield: 12 muffins

Beth Page
Washington

Saturday Morning Feather Pancakes

1 1/4	cup sifted all-purpose flour
1	tablespoon baking powder
1	tablespoon sugar
1/2	teaspoon salt
1	egg, beaten
1	cup milk (a little more if you like thin cakes)
2	tablespoons cooking oil

Sift together flour, baking powder, sugar, and salt. Combine egg, milk, and cooking oil; add to dry ingredients, stirring just until flour is moistened (batter will be lumpy). Cook on hot griddle at 350 degrees.

Yield: 8 pancakes

Sallie Scales
Washington

French Breakfast Muffins

5	tablespoons butter
1/2	cup sugar
1	egg
1 1/2	cups all-purpose flour
2	teaspoons baking powder
1/4	teaspoon salt
1/4	teaspoon nutmeg
1/2	cup milk

Cream butter and sugar. Add egg. Mix well. Add sifted dry ingredients alternately with milk. Fill miniature greased muffin tins 2/3 full. Bake at 350 degrees for 15 minutes. When done, take out of pan immediately and coat.

Coating

6	tablespoons butter, melted
1/2	cup sugar
1	teaspoon cinnamon

Mix sugar and cinnamon. Roll hot muffins in butter, then sugar mixture. These can be reheated in foil if needed. The muffins freeze well.

Yield: 24 muffins

Another winner! Reheats well.

Beth Page
Washington

German Oven Pancake

6	eggs
1/4	cup melted margarine
3/4	teaspoon salt
1	cup milk
1	cup all-purpose flour
6	teaspoons butter or margarine
	confectioners' sugar

Combine all ingredients in a blender and blend well. Stir the flour in a little bit first. When smooth, pour into a 9x13-inch greased baking dish, and bake in a 450 degree oven for 20 minutes. The pancake will be all puffed up. Take it out, drizzle melted margarine on it, and sprinkle it with confectioners' sugar. Serve immediately.

Yield: 4 to 6 servings

This is so fun for kids! They love to see how it puffs up, and it's a nice alternative to regular pancakes. You do not need syrup as the pancake is very moist.

Jan De Hoog
Terra Ceia

The story that goes with these global crêpes is that when I was eight I stayed at a German neighbour's house. I was fed "German Pancakes" for breakfast. When I got home, I told my Grandmother Nilsen what I had had. She said I had had Norwegian pancakes, not German. She taught me how to make them right then. I have cooked these pancakes while we have traveled the world or had guests visit us. It is amazing how each nationality uses basically the same idea but has different toppings. Of course the French try to claim the crêpe, but it is our experience that this fun way to start a day is really a wonderfully global food.

Not as complicated as it sounds and fun to try a global mix!

Norwegian Pancakes (Global Crêpes)

1 egg per person, plus,
1 egg "for the pot" for each four persons,
    ie: 3 persons= 3+1 eggs, 6 persons= 6+2 eggs
    milk, 1/2% to whole milk will work
    all-purpose flour
    vegetable cooking spray
    margarine, squeeze container
    jams, jellies, syrup, etc.

Crack eggs into blender. With fingers on the side of the blender, measure the egg volume. Move bottom finger to top of egg volume and add milk to the level of the moved upper finger. Really what you are doing is adding as much milk as you have egg volume. Blend at low speed. With blender running at low speed, add 2 level tablespoons of flour per egg. Mix until all the flour is blended in. Let the mixture stand about ten minutes to reduce the amount of bubbles. What you want out of all this high tech measurement is a "runny" pancake mix!

Preheat an 8-inch non-stick fry pan and coat it with vegetable cooking spray. You don't want to have thin crêpes stick to the pan! Lift the pan from the stove and turn at a slight angle. Pour in enough mix (about 1/3 cup) so that when you swirl the pan the mix covers the bottom in a thin coat, like 1/8-inch thick.

As the crêpe cooks, take a plastic spatula and loosen the edges of the crêpe. When the crêpe "turns dry" the bottom is cooked. All the edge loosening lets you easily turn the crêpe over. Squeeze on a few swirls of margarine and use the spatula to spread the margarine over the crêpe as the second side cooks. Cooking time per pancake depends on the stove burner heat, but these crêpes do not take long to cook. Remove the crêpe from the pan and place it on a heated plate. Cook up all the crêpes so all the folks can eat together and see who makes what kind of Global Crêpe!

Serving is best done with the "use your fingers to pick one up" method. Once you get a crêpe on your plate, spread one of the "nationality condiments" on the crêpe, then roll the crêpe into a "log", using your knife and fork. Cut across the log so you get a "roll up" piece of crêpe and condiment.

Condiments for Global Crêpes:

Norwegian pancakes, use strawberry jelly or jam.

Scottish pancakes, use sprinkled confectioners' sugar moistened with fresh lemon juice from slices.

(continued)

German pancakes, use apple butter.

Vermont crêpes, use maple syrup

North Carolina pancakes, use blueberry jam.

Bajan pancakes, use guava jelly.

Italian pancakes, use chocolate hazelnut spread.

Dieter pancakes, use cottage cheese and peach slices.

Russian Blini pancakes, use sour cream blended with sugar.

Jewish blintzes, use a similar sour cream blend.

You can use left over pancakes for lunch with a tuna salad spread, or for dessert with soft ice cream spread and chocolate sauce!

Richard Seale
Washington

Gingery Banana Waffles

1 1/2   cups all-purpose flour
2   teaspoons baking powder
3/4   teaspoon salt
1   teaspoon cinnamon
3/4   teaspoon ground ginger
2   eggs
1/3   cup brown sugar
3/4   cup milk
1/4   cup molasses
1   ripe banana, mashed
1/4   cup butter, melted
2   large bananas, sliced

In a medium mixing bowl, combine flour, baking powder, salt and spices. In another bowl, beat eggs with sugar until light and fluffy. Stir in milk, molasses and mashed banana. Add all at once to dry ingredients and stir until moistened. Stir in melted butter. Bake in waffle iron to a deep golden brown. Serve with sliced bananas and syrup, if desired.

Yield: 5 8-inch waffles.

Sue Mansfield
Washington

Pecan Waffles with Apple-Cinnamon Syrup

2	eggs, beaten
2	cups buttermilk
1	teaspoon baking soda
2	cups sifted all-purpose flour
2	teaspoons baking powder
1/2	teaspoon salt
6	tablespoons vegetable oil
1/3	cup pecans, coarsely chopped

Heat waffle iron while mixing the batter.

Add buttermilk to eggs, whisk, then add dry ingredients and oil. Stir nuts in last. Whisk until smooth. Bake in a hot waffle iron according to manufacturer's instructions.

For garnish, thinly slice quartered red-skinned apple (Rome Beauty, MacIntosh, etc.) and place five slices, cartwheel fashion, on finished waffle.

Serve with warm apple-cinnamon syrup.

Yield: 5 Waffles (doubles easily - 12 tablespoons oil = 3/4 cup)

Jane Fields
Washington

Find apple-cinnamon syrup in gourmet food shops.

Sam Wall III

Jayne On Pier

oil

Vegetables & Side Dishes

Artichoke Marinara

2	tablespoons olive oil
2 to 4	garlic cloves
	fresh parsley, handful
1/2 to 2/3	(2-ounce) tin anchovies or paste
1	(26-ounce) can tomatoes, chopped
1	sprig fresh basil, torn
1	teaspoon oregano
1	(14-ounce) can artichoke hearts
1	teaspoon sugar (optional)
	pasta, cooked

Almost cover bottom of sauce pan with olive oil. Add 2 to 4 garlic cloves, then chopped parsley. Add anchovies, tomatoes, basil and oregano after the garlic cloves become transparent. Add 1 can artichoke hearts cut into bite-sized pieces. Add a teaspoon of sugar for taste (optional). Simmer 30 minutes. Serve over your favorite cooked pasta.

Yield: 4 servings

Frances Lassiter
Washington Park

Always Perfect Asparagus

2	pounds fresh asparagus
1	tablespoon lemon juice
4	tablespoons fresh parsley, minced
	salt and pepper to taste
2	tablespoons unsalted butter, melted
2	tablespoons olive oil

Preheat oven to 400 degrees. Wash and drain asparagus. Snap off ends. Arrange asparagus in single layer of 9x13-inch glass baking dish. Sprinkle lemon juice over asparagus. Sprinkle with parsley, salt and pepper. Combine melted butter and olive oil and drizzle over asparagus. Cover with foil and bake 15 minutes. Uncover and sprinkle with fresh parsley.

Yield: 8 servings

Ruth Pugh
Washington

Use fresh asparagus only. Never fear overcooking asparagus when it is prepared this way!

Broccoli and Rice Casserole

This dish was served with great success at the Beaufort County Arts Council's lunch for the Raleigh Fine Arts Society in December 2000.

2	cups rice, cooked
1	(8-ounce) block cheddar cheese, cubed
2	(10-ounce) packages frozen broccoli cuts, cooked and drained
1	can cream of chicken soup
1	can water chestnuts, sliced and drained
1/2	cup milk
1	teaspoon Worcestershire sauce
	salt and pepper to taste
	bread crumbs

Combine hot rice and broccoli with cheese. Allow cheese to melt before adding other ingredients. Place in buttered casserole. Sprinkle top with bread crumbs. Bake at 350 degrees for 20 to 30 minutes.

Yield: 8 servings

Alice McClure
Washington

Broccoli Macaroni Bake

In the early 1900s, a dish of macaroni was served only in the winter. It showed poor taste to have macaroni in the summer.

2	cups broccoli, cooked
1 3/4	cups macaroni, cooked (1 1/4 cups uncooked)
3	tablespoons butter
3	tablespoons all-purpose flour
1 1/2	teaspoons salt
1/2	teaspoon pepper
1 1/2	cups milk
1/2 to 3/4	cup mayonnaise
	cheddar cheese, grated

Cook broccoli and drain. Cook macaroni and drain. Melt butter in large frying pan and stir in flour. Add salt and pepper, and then add milk slowly, cooking until thick. Add mayonnaise and mix well. In greased 1 1/2-quart casserole, layer broccoli and macaroni. Pour sauce over all and cover with grated cheese. Bake at 350 degrees for 30 minutes.

Yield: 8 servings

Steven Deans
Aurora

Broccoli Casserole

2	(10-ounce) packages frozen chopped broccoli, cooked and drained
1	cup sharp cheddar cheese, shredded
1	can cream of mushroom soup
1	medium onion, chopped
2	eggs
1	cup mayonnaise
1/2	cup water chestnuts, chopped (optional)
1	(8-ounce) package herbed poultry stuffing mix
3	tablespoons butter, melted

Mix ingredients (except herbed stuffing mix and butter) together in order listed. Pour into a buttered 3-quart casserole dish. Top with herbed poultry stuffing which has been mixed with butter. Bake at 350 degrees for 30 minutes.

Yield: 6 servings

Burkely Gorham, Bea Simmons, Mary C. Hull, Ruth Edwards
Washington

Two Beans and a Pea

1	(10-ounce) package frozen lima beans
1	(10-ounce) package frozen french green beans
1	(10-ounce) package frozen green peas
1	cup mayonnaise
1	medium purple onion, chopped
1	teaspoon prepared mustard
1	teaspoon Worcestershire sauce
1	small can water chestnuts, sliced (drained)
	bread crumbs, buttered

Cook the beans and peas according to package directions. Mix the remaining ingredients and add to beans. Pour into a greased 2-quart casserole dish. Cover with buttered bread crumbs and bake at 350 degrees until top browns and edges begin to bubble.

Yield: 6 to 8 servings

Anne Stuart Rumley
Washington

Sweet and Sour Green Beans

A different taste for green beans.

2	pound green beans, fresh or 3 (9-ounce) packages, frozen
1	cup water
2	slices bacon
1/2	cup diced onion
1	tablespoon all-purpose flour
1/4	cup white vinegar
2	tablespoons sugar
1	teaspoon salt
1/4	teaspoon pepper

Boil water and add washed beans. Cook 10 minutes, drain and reserve 3/4 cup liquid. Cook bacon, remove and sauté onions in bacon grease until tender. Add flour and cook 1 minute, stirring. Stir in reserved liquid and seasonings. Simmer 8 to 10 minutes or until thickened, stirring. Add beans, toss and heat. Top with crumbled bacon.

Yield: 8 servings

Helen Myers
Pantego

Nutty Cabbage

"Cabbage-comes-to-dinner recipe."

1	teaspoon instant beef bouillon granules
1/4	cup water
5	cups coarsely shredded cabbage
1	cup coarsely shredded carrots
1/2	cup sliced green onions
1/2	teaspoon salt (optional)
2	tablespoons margarine, melted
1	tablespoon prepared mustard
1/3	cup chopped pecans (or more, to taste)

In 12-inch fry pan, heat water and bouillon until dissolved. Add all the vegetables, mix well and cover. Cook over medium heat 5 to 10 minutes, or until tender. Stir once during cooking. Drain, if necessary. In a small pan, melt margarine, stirring in the mustard and pecans. Pour over vegetables. Toss to mix well. Place in serving dish.

Yield: 6 servings

Louise Lane
Washington

Kathy's Cabbage Casserole

2	cups crushed cornflakes
4 to 5	cups shredded cabbage
2	small cans water chestnuts, sliced and drained
1	medium onion, chopped
1	stick margarine, melted
1	can cream of celery soup
1	cup milk
1/2	cup mayonnaise
4 to 6	ounces cheddar cheese, shredded

Spray a 13x9-inch pan with non-stick spray. Layer 1 cup of cornflakes, cabbage, water chestnuts and onions. Mix margarine, soup, milk, mayonnaise and pour over mixture. Cover with cheddar cheese and remaining cup of cornflakes. Cook at 350 degrees for 1 hour.

Yield: 8 to 10 servings

Katherine Adams
Washington Park

The South's favorite, a dish of collards, is not difficult to prepare. Just put a ham hock into a pot with water to cover. Let simmer about 2 hours. Meanwhile, wash collards well, remove hard stems, then place all in the same pot. Extra water is not needed, as leaves will shrink as they begin to cook. Cover, cook until tender, about 30 minutes. Remove, drain and chop lightly. Serve with hot pepper vinegar. Collards are at their best and cook faster after frost has "struck" them.

Creamed Celery

2	tablespoons butter
3	tablespoons all-purpose flour
2	cups milk
4	cups celery, cut in 1/2 inch pieces
1	teaspoon salt
1/2	teaspoon paprika
1/2	cup pecans
3/4	cup bread crumbs

Make white sauce by melting the butter and stirring in the flour. Add milk slowly, stirring until sauce is smooth. Add salt, paprika and celery to sauce. Put in 1 1/2-quart casserole. Top with pecans and bread crumbs. Bake at 400 degrees for 15 minutes.

Yield: 4 to 6 servings

Mavis Rodman Peele
Washington

A new look at celery.

Sunshine Carrots

1/4 cup plus 2 tablespoons orange juice
1/4 cup maple syrup
2 tablespoons orange marmalade
2 (16-ounce) cans small whole carrots, drained

Combine first 3 ingredients in saucepan. Bring to boil, stirring constantly. Add carrots. Return to boil. Reduce heat to low. Cook 5 minutes.

Yield: 4 servings

Alice C. Elks
Belhaven

Corn Pudding

The favorite food of the late Murray Hamilton, Washington native and noted actor, was a big bowl of butterbeans and corn.

1 stick butter
2 tablespoons all-purpose flour
1/2 cup sugar
1 cup milk
2 eggs, beaten
1 (15 1/4-ounce) can of cream-style corn
1 (8 1/4-ounce) can of cream-style corn

Melt butter in 9x13-inch casserole dish. Combine sugar and flour. Add milk and beaten eggs. Stir in corn. Pour mixture into casserole dish with melted butter. Bake at 350 degrees until custard is set and top is golden brown, approximately 1 hour and 5 minutes.

Yield: 8 servings

Nancy J. Lilley
Washington

Corn on the Cob

8 to 10	ears fresh corn
3 to 4	quarts water
1/4 to 1/2	cup sugar
1	cup milk (at least)

Remove husks and silks from corn just before cooking. Combine water, sugar and milk in a Dutch oven. Stir to dissolve sugar. Bring water to a boil and add corn. Return to a boil and cook 8 to 10 minutes until tender. Drain well. Serve immediately.

Yield: 8 to 10 servings

Note: You can pre-soak corn in a mixture of milk, sugar and water. You may freeze fresh unhusked corn. Pull down husk just to expose silk, remove silks and pull husks back up. Freeze in a cotton pillowcase in freezer for months. However, this is still not as good as fresh!!

Pamela Gunnin Burkart
Washington

At the North Carolina State Fair years ago a civic club had a corn-on-the-cob concession. My friend and I ate a dozen ears each. The men serving this corn gave us their "secret." When I serve it my family turns into "piglets."

Corn Oyster "Flitters"

1	cup corn
1	egg
1/4	cup all-purpose flour
1/4	teaspoon baking powder
1/2	teaspoon salt
1/2	teaspoon sugar

Grate raw corn from cob or use canned corn. To corn pulp, add well-beaten egg, flour, baking powder, salt and sugar. Drop by spoon into deep or shallow fat. Batter spreads out to look like an oyster. Drain on paper towels and serve.

Yield: 8 to 10 servings

Mildred Rumley
Washington Park

These are light and delicious! "Flitters" is a Beaufort County name for fritters.

Corn Fritters

2	cups fresh corn, may use frozen
3	eggs, separated
1/2	teaspoon salt
1/2	teaspoon pepper
1/4	cup all-purpose flour
1/4	cup milk

Separate eggs; beat yolks and stir in rest of ingredients except the egg whites. Beat egg whites until stiff and fold in last. Fry in very hot oil.

Yield: 12 to 15 servings

Tay Carter
Washington

Be careful - they pop! These fritters spread out like lace-edged cornbread.

Eggplant Fritters

2 to 3 eggplants, medium or larger

Peel and cut each eggplant into finger strips about 1/4 to 1/2-inch thick. Sprinkle with salt and allow to sit about 20 minutes. Then drain in colander. Do not break strips. Lay on paper towels and pat dry.

Batter

(Make while draining eggplant)

1	cup all-purpose flour
1	teaspoon baking powder
1/2	teaspoon salt
	dash of pepper
2	eggs, beaten
2/3	cup cold milk
1	tablespoon salad oil (canola)

Mix all together until smooth. Dip eggplant strips into batter. Drop the strips, a few at a time directly into deep, medium hot fat. Remove with slotted spoon and drain on paper towels. Keep warm until all strips are done. Sprinkle lightly with confectioners' sugar to serve.

Note: Any batter left over can be refrigerated and used the next day.

Yield: 6 servings

My family eats these faster than I can get them to the table!

Connie Howard
Washington

Easy Vegetable Casserole

2	cans asparagus
1	pound fresh squash, sliced
3	potatoes, peeled and cut in chunks
1/2	cup water
1/2	pound sharp cheddar cheese, cut into strips
1/2	teaspoon salt
1/2	teaspoon pepper
	bread crumbs
	parsley flakes
1/2	cup grated cheddar cheese

In a 9x13-inch casserole, place asparagus in a center line. On one side, place the squash slices, and on opposite side, place the potato chunks. Add water so that it covers the bottom of the casserole. Separate the vegetables with strips of sharp cheese. Sprinkle salt and pepper over vegetables. A light covering of parsley flakes, bread crumbs and grated cheese will enhance the flavor. Cover tightly with foil and bake at 350 degrees for 30 to 40 minutes.

Yield: 6 servings

Mary Alice Chapin
Washington

"Those Potatoes"

10	potatoes, peeled
1	tablespoon butter
3	tablespoons all-purpose flour
1	cup half and half (may use low-fat)
1	cup chicken stock
3/4	cup Parmesan cheese
	blue cheese (at least 2 ounces, or to taste)
	salt, to taste

This is a great side dish with lamb or beef. We like it when we have company or on other special occasions.

Cook potatoes in salted water, approximately 20 minutes. Drain and cube. Melt butter, add flour and make a roux. Over low heat, add half and half and chicken stock slowly, stirring constantly. When thick, add Parmesan cheese. Pour roux over cooked potatoes that have been placed in a 9x13-inch glass baking dish. Dot with butter and blue cheese. Bake at 350 degrees for 30 minutes or until bubbling.

Yield: 8 to 10 servings

Catherine Partrick
Washington

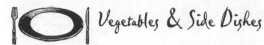
Braised Peppers and Potatoes Italiano

Colorful and good! You may also add Polish sausage if you like. Add this near the end of cooking. With the addition of sausage, this would be a good entrée.

6	large peppers, red and green
3	medium onions
4	medium potatoes, skins on
1/2	pound mushrooms, fresh
1/4	cup olive oil
2	garlic cloves, crushed
1/4	cup water
2	tablespoons red wine vinegar
1	teaspoon chicken bouillon
3/4	teaspoon salt
1	teaspoon fresh basil, chopped (or 1/2 teaspoon dried)
	parsley for garnish

Cut peppers (3 red, 3 green) into 1/2 inch strips. Cut onions into quarters. Cut potatoes in 1/2 inch slices. If mushrooms are large, cut into halves. In 12-inch skillet, heat oil over medium heat, then cook all vegetables and garlic until lightly browned. Stir gently and often during cooking. Then stir in water, vinegar, bouillon, salt and basil. Heat until boiling. Reduce heat to low, cover and simmer about 15 to 20 minutes, stirring occasionally. Test with fork for tenderness. Place on platter and garnish with parsley sprigs.

Yield: 6 servings

Connie Howard
Washington

Potato Farls

This is a good way to use leftover mashed potatoes.

A farl is defined as a thin Scottish griddle cake shaped in wedges.

2	cup mashed potatoes
1	cup all-purpose flour
	salt
	bacon grease

Mix well potatoes and flour. Make cakes and fry in bacon grease until golden brown. Sprinkle with salt.

Alice Norman
Aurora

Scalloped Potatoes

6	large baking potatoes
6	slices bacon
2	medium onions, thinly sliced
1	tablespoon all-purpose flour
1 1/2	cups milk
1/2	teaspoon salt, over each layer
1/4	teaspoon pepper, over each layer

Peel potatoes and cut into thin slices. Fry bacon in skillet just until rendered and bacon is limp. Remove bacon and set aside. Sauté onion slices in bacon fat until limp (this step isn't essential but improves the flavor). Mix flour with about 2 tablespoons of the milk, then whisk into milk. In a deep, buttered casserole, layer about one third of the potatoes. Top with half the onion and three slices of bacon. Pour one third of milk/flour mixture over layer. Sprinkle with salt and pepper. Repeat layers. Top with remaining potatoes. Pour remaining milk mixture over and sprinkle with salt and pepper. Cover and bake at 375 degrees for about an hour or until potatoes are tender. Uncover for last 15 minutes of baking, allowing potatoes on top to brown. Let sit about 10 minutes before serving.

Yield: 6 to 8 servings

Harriet W. O'Neal
Belhaven

Sweet Potatoes and Apples

5	medium sweet potatoes
5	medium apples
1/2	cup butter
1	cup sugar
1/2 to 1	cup water
2	tablespoons lemon juice

Boil sweet potatoes and cut into thick slices. Core apples; slice thickly. Place alternating layers of sweet potato slices and apple slices in a 9x13-inch baking dish. Dot with butter and sprinkle with sugar. Pour hot water and lemon juice over mixture. Bake at 375 degrees for 30 minutes.

Yield: 10 servings

Christine Jackson
Pinetown

Rachel Futrell
Washington

Martha McRoy
Chocowinity

Taken from a 1920s newspaper article:

"Aurora, Beaufort County, NC, is located on South Creek, 6 miles from the Pamlico River and is the largest town on the Washington and Vandermere Railroad and the largest shipping point. The town shipped in one year 4,500 bales of cotton, more than 70,000 barrels of potatoes and from 1,200 to 1,500 cases of eggs…" In the late 1920s, 30s and early 40s, Aurora was known as "Potato Capital of the World."

I make this recipe at Christmas all the time. I am always asked to make it.

Sweet Potatoes de Mere

4	large sweet potatoes (8 to 10 medium potatoes)
1	(8-ounce) box crushed and divided corn flakes
1	cup broken pecan meats
1 1/2	tablespoons all-purpose flour
1/2	cup sugar (more if needed)
2	tablespoons milk
1	teaspoon cinnamon
1	teaspoon vanilla
1/2	teaspoon baking powder
1	egg

These are delicious! A nice change from the usual potato casserole.

Boil potatoes until soft. Drain and peel; mash until smooth. Add 1 cup crushed cornflakes and remaining ingredients (taste for seasoning before adding egg). Mix well. Shape into balls about 1 1/2 inches in diameter. Roll in additional crushed cornflake crumbs (total crumbs will be almost an 8-ounce box of cornflakes). Place on wax paper-lined cookie sheet to set. Fry in hot deep fat. Drain and serve. May be cooked, frozen, reheated in oven; or may be frozen, then cooked. Very good to have on hand for a quick dish or a large crowd.

Yield: 75 balls, 20 to 30 servings

Connie Howard
Washington

Okra and Fresh Corn Casserole

3	cups okra, cut
2	tablespoons butter or margarine
6	ears fresh corn or 2 (10-ounce) packages frozen whole kernel corn
	salt and pepper to taste
2	tablespoons butter or margarine
2	tablespoons all-purpose flour
1	cup milk
1/4	pound shredded sharp cheddar cheese
1	cup bread or cracker crumbs

Remember the James Tea Room on Second Street in Washington? It later moved to the corner of Second and Bridge and had delicious home-cooked meals.

Wash okra and drain well. Place in skillet with 2 tablespoons butter and let cook slowly, stirring frequently until the sticky substance disappears. Cut corn from cob. Put okra and corn in alternate layers in a greased 8x10-inch casserole. Sprinkle with salt and pepper. Make a sauce with 2 tablespoons butter, flour and milk. Stir well. Do not let roux brown. Add cheese and stir until melted. Pour over okra and corn. Cover with crumbs. Bake at 350 degrees for about 30 minutes or until top is slightly brown.

Yield: 6 servings

Gayle Morgan
Washington Park

Spinach and Artichoke Casserole

1   (8-ounce) package cream cheese
1   stick butter
2   tablespoons lemon juice
1   (14-ounce) can artichoke hearts, cut up
3   (10-ounce) boxes frozen spinach, cooked and drained
    breadcrumbs
    grated cheese

A great combination of flavors!

Mix cream cheese and butter in pan on low heat. Add lemon juice. When this has all melted, add spinach and artichokes and mix well. Place in 2-quart casserole. Top with breadcrumbs and grated cheese. Bake at 350 degrees until bubbling.

Yield: 8 servings

Athy Cooper
Washington

Laundromat Spinach

2   (10-ounce) packages frozen spinach, chopped
1   can water chestnuts, drained
1   cup sour cream
1   cup mayonnaise
1   package dried vegetable soup mix

For "company," a dozen or so crushed round buttery crackers to border the dish looks festive.

I copied this delicious recipe directly from the grocery store receipt on which my mother had jotted it down while talking to a total stranger at a Durham laundromat.

Undercook spinach, using directions on box. Drain well and pat dry on paper towels. Combine with remaining ingredients and pour into baking dish. Bake at 350 degrees, uncovered, for 20 to 25 minutes or until bubbly.

Yield: 6 servings

Kaye Mayer
Washington

Spinach Madelaine

2	(10-ounce) packages frozen chopped spinach
4	tablespoons butter
2	tablespoons all-purpose flour
2	tablespoons chopped onion
1/2	cup evaporated milk
1/2	cup vegetable liquor
1/2	teaspoon pepper
3/4	teaspoon celery salt
3/4	teaspoon garlic salt
6	ounces pepper cheese, cut in small pieces
1	teaspoon Worcestershire sauce

A versatile dish, and especially pretty served as stuffing for whole tomatoes.

Cook spinach and drain well. Save vegetable liquor. Melt butter over low heat. Add flour and stir until smooth. Add onion and cook until soft. Add milk and spinach liquor (1/2 cup), stirring constantly until smooth and thick. Add seasonings and cheese. Stir until cheese is melted. Add cooked spinach. Blend well. Can be served immediately or put in 2-quart casserole. Top with buttered bread crumbs. The flavor is better if it sits overnight in refrigerator. This can be frozen or can be used in whole, stuffed tomatoes. Bake at 375 to 400 degrees for 20 to 30 minutes.

Yield: 5 to 6 servings

Rosemarie Edwards
Washington Park

Browned Down Summer Squash

8	medium summer squash
3	large onions
3	tablespoons cooking oil
	salt and pepper, to taste

This recipe has been in our family for over 100 years. Originally, the oil called for was either lard or fried meat grease. The secret to goodness is browning to bring out the sweetness of the squash.

Wash squash and slice. Slice onions. In iron frying pan (do not use non-stick pan), put 3 tablespoons oil. Then add squash and onions. Do not cover until squash shrinks down. Cook on medium until tender. Stir to prevent sticking. Allow liquid to evaporate. Cover and cook until you attain desired color. Serve hot.

Yield: 6 servings

Lillian W. Hopkins
Washington

Summer Squash Oregano

3	tablespoons butter, melted
1	onion, sliced
1	garlic clove, minced
1	green pepper, chopped
1	tablespoon fresh oregano
3/4	pound squash, sliced
3/4	pound zucchini, sliced
4	tomatoes, chopped
	salt and pepper
	Parmesan cheese

Sauté onion, garlic and green pepper in butter until tender. Stir in oregano, squash and zucchini and tomatoes. Sprinkle Parmesan cheese lightly over top. Cover and cook 15 minutes. Stir occasionally.

Yield: 6 servings

Mary Emily Moore
Washington

Hester Anne's Pasta and Veggie Bonnie

assorted garden vegetables (or whatever you have in your refrigerator)
angel hair pasta, cooked
olive oil
Italian dressing

Stir fry in small amount of olive oil whatever vegetables you have, for example, celery, snow peas, carrots, red and green bell peppers and yellow squash.

Cook angel hair pasta. Drain and stir in small amount of Italian dressing. Mix vegetables and pasta together.

Yield: 4 servings

Hester Anne Kidd
Washington

This recipe was made from things I had in my refrigerator when Hurricane Bonnie came through.

Bonnie blew in a good dish!

Vegetable Lasagna

	Marinara Sauce, 2 recipes
	lasagna noodles, double layer to fit pan
2	(10-ounce) packages frozen spinach, thawed and water removed
3	carrots, grated
1	(8-ounce) package portabella or button mushrooms (canned may be substituted)
2	medium zucchini, sliced
1/2	teaspoon Italian seasoning herbs
1/2	teaspoon olive oil
3 to 4	cups mozzarella cheese, grated
1/4 to 1/2	cup Parmesan cheese, grated
1	(16-ounce) container cottage cheese

A delicious, easy and lowfat sauce for a variety of pasta creations! Easily doubles. Chopped onions, additional olive oil and garlic may be added to taste.

Marinara Sauce

1/2	tablespoon olive oil
1	small clove elephant garlic
1	(14 1/2-ounce) can Italian-style tomatoes
1	(15-ounce) can tomato sauce
1	(6-ounce) can tomato paste
1/2	cup water or red wine
1 1/2	teaspoon dried basil
1/4	teaspoon dried oregano
1	bay leaf
1/8	cup sugar
1/4	teaspoon salt
1/4 to 1/2	teaspoon freshly ground mixed peppercorns

Prepare marinara sauce. In heavy, large saucepan, heat olive oil over low heat. Add garlic and sauté for about 30 seconds, being careful not to brown. Add remaining ingredients and mix well. Simmer, partially covered, for 1 hour. Discard bay leaf.

Cook lasagna noodles as package directs. Heat olive oil over medium heat. Add Italian herbs and vegetables. Lightly sauté vegetables. In an oiled 9x13-inch pan, assemble lasagna in following order: sauce to cover pan bottom, noodles, cottage cheese, vegetables, sauce and cheeses, and repeat. The amount of cheese is a matter of taste and diet preference. Bake at 350 degrees until heated through, approximately 1 1/2 hours. Cover loosely with foil at appropriate time during baking to prevent over-browning.

Yield: 6 to 8 servings

Wanda Johnson
Washington

Curried Rice

1	cup rice, uncooked
2	tablespoons chopped green pepper
1	small onion, chopped
1	can beef consommé
1	soup can water
1	teaspoon salt
1	teaspoon curry powder
1/2	teaspoon chili powder
1	tablespoon parsley flakes

Cook rice, green pepper and onion in a skillet with no oil, stirring continuously to prevent sticking, until rice browns. Add consommé, water, salt, chili powder, curry powder and parsley. Cover the pot and bring to a boil. Turn down to simmer and cook, covered, approximately 25 minutes, or until liquid is absorbed.

Yield: 4 servings

Mary Baade
Washington

Venetian Peas and Rice

4	slices bacon
3	tablespoons butter
1	small onion, diced
1	(10-ounce) package frozen peas
3/4	cup regular rice, uncooked
2	cans chicken broth
1/4	cup grated Parmesan cheese
1	teaspoon salt
	dash of pepper

This is one of my very favorite recipes. I use it with anything but fish.

Using a heavy skillet, sauté bacon until crisp. Remove and dice bacon. Pour off fat; add butter and onion to the same skillet and sauté. Stir in peas and rice and stir until well coated with butter. Stir in 2 cups of canned broth, salt and pepper. Simmer covered, about 20 minutes, stirring occasionally, until rice absorbs all liquid and is tender. Toss with grated cheese and crisp bacon.

Yield: 4 servings

Jean Duke Trueblood
Washington

Vidalia Onion Pie

1	cup finely crumbled round buttery crackers
1/2	stick butter, melted
2	cups thinly sliced Vidalia onions
2	tablespoons butter
2	eggs
3/4	cup milk
	parsley
	black pepper
	dash Tabasco sauce
1/2	cup grated cheese
	paprika

Trust me, it is delicious.

Mix cracker crumbs with melted butter. Press into 8-inch pie plate to form pie crust. Sauté onions in 2 tablespoons butter. Spoon into crust. Beat eggs with milk. Add parsley, pepper and Tabasco sauce. Pour over onions. Top with cheese and sprinkle with paprika. Bake at 350 degrees for about 30 minutes.

Yield: 6 servings

Hazel Lassiter
Mary Emily Moore
Washington

Baked Stuffed Mushrooms

8	large mushroom caps
1	tablespoon lemon juice
1/2	teaspoon instant minced onion
1/2	teaspoon water
1/3 to 1/2	cup herb-seasoned stuffing mix
2	strips bacon, cooked crisp, crumbled
	chicken stock

Preheat oven to 350 degrees. Wash mushrooms, remove stems. Brush caps with lemon juice. Set aside. Mix minced onion with water. Let stand 5 minutes to soften. Chop mushroom stems and sauté 3 to 4 minutes in bacon fat with onion. Add stuffing, bacon and enough chicken broth to moisten. Stuff caps and place in a 9-inch round, glass baking dish. Add a little chicken broth to cover bottom of dish. Cook 8 to 10 minutes. Serve hot.

Yield: 4 servings

Judy Kidwell
Washington

Mushroom Pilaf

1/2   cup butter (1 stick) or margarine
1 1/2 cups regular rice (not instant)
1   can condensed beef consommé
1   can condensed French onion soup
1/2   pound mushrooms, trimmed and sliced
1 1/2 cups shredded cheddar cheese

Note: You may use canned mushrooms. If you do, drain well.

Spray 2-quart casserole dish with vegetable cooking spray. Melt butter in casserole and stir in rice to coat grains. Add soup, consommé and mushrooms. Mix well. Cover and bake at 325 degrees for about 55 minutes, or until rice is tender and liquid is absorbed. Stir occasionally during baking period. Remove cover, top with cheddar cheese and return to oven for 5 more minutes.

Yield: 6 servings

Ann and Ray Wiseman
Chocowinity

Tomato Tarts

4   individual pie shells
4   fresh tomatoes, enough to fill shells
2   heaping tablespoons mayonnaise
2   heaping tablespoons sour cream
       cheddar cheese, grated
       salt and pepper, optional

Bake pie shells. Cut up tomatoes. Squeeze out as much juice as possible. Put tomatoes in shells. Mix mayonnaise and sour cream. Spoon over tomatoes. Sprinkle cheese on top. Bake at 350 degrees until hot and cheese is melted.

Yield: 4 servings

Mary W. Payne
Washington

Very nice for a book club luncheon.

Tomato Pie

1	9-inch pie shell, deep dish, pre-baked for 5 minutes
5	large tomatoes, peeled and sliced thick
1/2	teaspoon salt
1/2	teaspoon pepper
3	teaspoons dried basil
	garlic powder to taste
3/4	cup mayonnaise
1 1/4	cups grated cheddar cheese

Layer tomatoes in pie shell and sprinkle each layer with salt, pepper, basil and garlic powder which have been combined. Combine mayonnaise and cheese and spread on tomatoes. Bake at 350 degrees for 35 minutes. Check crust and cover edge with foil. Set 5 minutes before serving.

Yield: 8 servings

Alva Douglas
Washington

Pinto Bean Pudding

Years ago, my mother-in-law gave me this recipe. She recently passed away at the age of 103. It is very good, much like bread pudding, and I would like to share it with others.

1/2	cup butter
1	egg
1	cup sugar
2	cups pinto beans, mashed well (canned may be substituted for fresh cooked)
1	cup all-purpose flour
2	teaspoons vanilla
1	teaspoon soda
1/4	teaspoon salt
1	teaspoon cinnamon
1	teaspoon allspice
1	teaspoon nutmeg
2	cups raisins
2	cups chopped apple

Beat all together until blended. Bake at 350 degrees for 45 minutes. Confectioners' sugar glaze, optional.

Yield: 6 servings

Joyce W. Moore
Chocowinity

Scalloped Pineapple

2   sticks margarine
2   cups sugar
3   eggs
1   (20-ounce) can crushed pineapple, drained, reserving juice
8   slices white bread, broken up

Cream margarine and sugar. Add eggs, then pineapple and bread. If mixture seems too dry, use some of the reserved pineapple juice. Pour into 9x13-inch baking dish. Bake at 350 degrees for about 45 minutes or until slightly brown. If too dry, add more juice. Can prepare ahead and put in refrigerator.

Charlene Alligood
Washington

Mary Jo Hatala
Chocowinity

Good served with ham.

Hot Fruit Compote

12   dried macaroons, crumbled
4   cups canned fruit (peaches, pears, apricots, pineapple chunks or
       cherries, well-drained)
1/2   cup brown sugar
1/2   cup cooking sherry
1/2   cup toasted almonds, slivered
1/4   cup butter, melted

Butter a 2 1/2-quart casserole. Cover bottom with macaroon crumbs. Arrange fruit on macaroons. Make another layer of macaroons and fruit. Finish with macaroons. Sprinkle with almonds, brown sugar and sherry. Bake at 350 degrees for 30 minutes. Add melted butter. Serve hot, as an accompaniment for a meat dish.

Yield: 6 servings

Kay Sharpe (in memory of her mother)
Washington

Macaroons really distinguish this dish.

River Forest Manor Tomato Casserole

1	(20-ounce) can whole tomatoes
3/4	teaspoon salt
2	tablespoons butter
1	cup toasted bread crumbs
1	large onion, chopped
1	tablespoon sugar

Mix all together and pour into 2-quart buttered casserole. Bake at 375 degrees for 15 to 20 minutes.

Yield: 4 servings

Melba G. Smith
River Forest Manor
Belhaven

Frans van Baars

Hog Killing

watercolor

Entrées

Barbecued Shrimp

3	strips of bacon, diced
2	tablespoons Dijon mustard
1/4	teaspoon basil
1/2	teaspoon Tabasco sauce
1	teaspoon black pepper
2	tablespoons crab boil
1/2	pound butter or margarine
1 1/2	teaspoons chili powder
1/4	teaspoon thyme
1/2	teaspoon oregano
2	cloves garlic, minced
1 1/2 to 2	pounds shrimp in shell, washed

Fry bacon until soft but not brown. Add all the other ingredients, except shrimp, and simmer for 5 minutes. Put shrimp in a 9x13-inch dish, pour mixture over it, stirring to cover, and bake at 375 degrees no longer than 15 to 20 minutes, stirring occasionally.

Yield: 4 to 6 servings

Shirley Padgett
Washington

Serve this with a pasta salad and lots of crusty bread and especially "finger bowls", as the shrimp are served in the shell and fingers do tend to get a bit messy!

Spicy Baked Shrimp

1/2	cup olive oil
2	tablespoons Cajun or Creole seasoning
2	tablespoons lemon juice
2	tablespoons chopped parsley
1	tablespoon honey
1	tablespoon soy sauce
	cayenne pepper
1	pound uncooked shrimp, peeled and deveined

Combine first 7 ingredients in 9x13-inch baking dish. Add shrimp. Refrigerate for 1 hour, or more. Bake at 450 degrees about 10 minutes, or until shrimp are cooked.

Yield: 4 servings

Mavis Rodman Peele
Washington

Shrimp with Artichokes

2	(14 1/2-ounce) cans artichoke hearts, drained
1	pound shrimp, cooked, peeled and deveined
1/2	pound fresh mushrooms, sliced
6	tablespoons butter
4	tablespoons all-purpose flour
1 1/2	cups milk
	salt and pepper to taste
1	tablespoon Worcestershire sauce
1/4	cup dry sherry
1	ounce Parmesan cheese, grated
	paprika
	fresh parsley

Preheat oven to 375 degrees. In bottom of a buttered casserole, arrange artichoke hearts. Spread shrimp over artichokes. Sauté mushrooms in 2 tablespoons butter for 6 minutes. Layer over shrimp. Melt remaining 4 tablespoons butter in a saucepan. Whisk in flour, stirring until well blended and smooth. Pour in milk, Worcestershire sauce and sherry, stirring until smooth and thickened. Pour over casserole. Sprinkle with cheese and paprika. Bake at 375 degrees for 30 to 40 minutes. Serve hot, garnished with an extra sprinkling of paprika and chopped, fresh parsley. Chicken may be substituted for shrimp.

Yield: 6 servings

Lorrie Beach
Washington

Shad Roe (non-splatter)

Cook 2 or 3 slices bacon, diced, in iron skillet. Carefully separate one set of roe. Salt and pepper each piece, put a pat of butter on each piece, and put onto separate sheets of waxed paper (just wide enough to double fold and long enough to twist with a couple of inches extra for handles). Remove bacon from pan and cook roe at medium heat in same pan, turning by handles to brown both sides, about 10 to 12 minutes. Paper will not burn, nor will roe break or split.

Yield: one set of roe, 6 servings

Nora Mae Griffin
Washington

Greek Shrimp and Leek Stir-Fry

1 1/4	pounds peeled and deveined shrimp
2/3	cup water
1/3	cup lemon juice
2	teaspoons cornstarch
1	tablespoon olive oil
4	leeks, cleaned and sliced thinly
1/4	cup chopped fresh Italian parsley
3	tablespoons minced fresh spicy basil
1	teaspoon snipped fresh thyme
1/2	cup crumbled feta cheese
1	small can sliced black olives

In a small bowl, combine and set aside the water, lemon juice and cornstarch. Stir-fry the leeks in the olive oil in a wok or large skillet until the leeks are tender, then remove them from the skillet and set them aside. Stir the lemon juice mixture. Add it to the skillet with the herbs and heat and stir until it boils. Add the shrimp and cook for about 3 minutes or until the shrimp turn pink. Stir in the leeks and half the feta cheese. Add salt to taste, if desired. Serve over cooked, hot rice or couscous. Top with olives and the remaining feta cheese.

Yield: 4 servings

Vera Van Camp
Washington

Shrimp and Pasta

2	pounds cleaned shrimp
2	tablespoons olive oil
2	cloves garlic, minced
	Cajun seafood seasoning
1	large bottle of light ranch dressing
	your favorite pasta

Sauté the garlic for a few minutes, add shrimp and sprinkle with a generous amount of seafood seasoning while the shrimp are still gray. Add the dressing (the entire bottle). Heat and serve over pasta.

Hester Anne Kidd
Washington

Delicious - a Kidd family favorite!

Sautéed Shrimp with Cheese Grits

Grits

1 1/2   cups chicken broth
1 1/2   cups milk
3/4   cup quick grits
1/4   teaspoon salt
1   cup shredded cheddar cheese

Shrimp

1   cup diced bacon
1   pound medium shrimp, peeled and deveined
1/2   cup thinly sliced strips green bell pepper
1/2   cup thinly sliced strips red bell pepper
1/2   cup slivered onion
       sliced green onions and shredded cheddar cheese for garnish
       Tabasco sauce

To prepare grits, bring chicken broth and milk to a boil in large saucepan. Stir in grits and salt; return to boil. Cover and reduce heat to low. Cook 5 minutes until thickened, stirring occasionally. Stir in cheddar cheese. Keep warm.

To prepare shrimp dish, cook bacon in skillet until crisp. Remove from skillet and drain bacon on paper towels; set aside. Drain all but 2 tablespoons drippings from skillet. Add shrimp, peppers and onion; cook until vegetables are tender and shrimp turns pink, about 3 to 5 minutes. Season with Tabasco sauce. Stir in bacon. Serve shrimp mixture over warm cheese grits. Garnish with chopped green onions and shredded Cheddar cheese.

Yield: 6 servings

Nancy Winfrey
Washington

Cajun Ham and Shrimp Jambalaya

6	tablespoons butter
1 1/2	cups - no less - chopped onions
3/4	cup finely sliced celery
1/3	cup finely chopped green pepper
2	tablespoons finely chopped garlic
1	(1-pound) can tomatoes, chopped (keep the liquid)
2 or 3	tablespoons chopped parsley
3	tablespoons tomato paste
4	whole cloves, pulverized with mortar and pestle
1	teaspoon dried thyme, crumbled
1/4 to 1/2	teaspoon ground cayenne pepper
	a few grinds of black pepper
1/2	pound good, Southern country ham, pre-cooked and cut into small cubes
2	pounds medium size shrimp, peeled and deveined
1	cup short grain rice
	salt to taste

Attention to detail makes this recipe. Soak ham to remove salt if ham is very salty. Short grain rice clumps together when cooked, the perfect rice for jambalaya.

Melt the butter in a big, deep, heavy frying pan or Dutch oven. Add the onion, celery, green pepper and garlic. Cook for about ten minutes over medium low fire, stirring constantly. Add the chopped tomatoes and the liquid you reserved. Add the cloves, parsley, tomato paste, thyme, cayenne and black pepper. Let this cook about an hour, no less, adding water as needed. It should bubble along at a slow boil. The final consistency, before you add the rice, ham and shrimp, should be good and moist but not too soupy. Add the diced ham and keep cooking and stirring for about 10 minutes.

While the vegetables are cooking, cook the rice until well-done.

All the above can be done well in advance, provided you can keep the rice hot. What comes next should be done just before you serve.

At the last minute, cook the shrimp in boiling water 3 minutes, removing them before water returns to boil. Heat the vegetable and ham mixture until it boils, then turn off the heat when the mixture is heated through and very hot. Add the shrimp. Stir well. Then add the rice and blend all together. Serve at once (from the same pan if possible - you don't want it to get cold and it should not be re-heated).

Yield: 4 to 6 servings

David Nash
Washington

Shrimp Creole

2	pounds fresh shrimp
2	tablespoons lemon juice
2	tablespoons Worcestershire sauce
2	teaspoons salt
3	tablespoons butter
1	medium-size onion, chopped
1/2	green pepper, chopped
1/2	cup chopped celery
1	clove garlic, minced
2	tablespoons all-purpose flour
1	teaspoon sugar
1/4	teaspoon pepper
2	dashes Tabasco sauce
2 1/4	cups canned or fresh tomatoes
8	ounces tomato sauce
2	cups cooked rice, buttered

Shell raw shrimp, devein, sprinkle shrimp with lemon, Worcestershire sauce and
1 teaspoon salt. Melt butter in large frying pan, add onion, green pepper, celery and
garlic and sauté over low heat about 5 minutes, or until vegetables are tender.
Blend flour, 1 teaspoon salt, sugar, pepper and Tabasco sauce into combined
tomatoes and tomato sauce. Cook covered over low heat 15 to 20 minutes or until
flavors are well-blended. Add seasoned raw shrimp; cover and cook over low heat
3 to 5 minutes, or until shrimp are firm. Serve over 2 cups hot buttered rice.

Yield: 8 servings

*Shields Harvey
Washington*

*Shields wrote for the
Greensboro Daily News
(Look Who's Cookin'!) in
1976; this was one of his
recipes.*

Shrimp Curry for a Crowd

1 1/2   cups butter
2 1/2   cups chopped onion
6   tablespoons chopped celery
2   cloves garlic, minced
1 1/2   teaspoons salt
3   tablespoons curry powder
1/3   cup all-purpose flour
3   cups milk
3   cups chicken broth
3   cups half and half
5 to 6   pounds shrimp, shelled, cleaned and cooked in salted water
6   tablespoons Madeira wine (or to taste)
   hot rice

Melt butter and sauté onions, celery and garlic for a few minutes. Do not brown. Add salt, curry powder and flour, mixing well. Slowly stir in liquids and simmer over low heat for 30 minutes. Check seasonings and refrigerate sauce overnight.

Nan Hawkins
Hawkins Beach

Start this recipe the day before your party. The flavors of the sauce blend and improve with overnight refrigeration. On party day, add shrimp and Madeira and reheat very slowly. Serve over hot rice

Shrimp, Crab and Wild Rice

1/4   cup diced onion
1/2   cup diced bell pepper
1/2   cup diced celery
2   pounds shrimp
1   pound crabmeat (or 3 cans crabmeat)
1   can water chestnuts, sliced
1   tablespoon Worcestershire sauce
   small jar sliced mushrooms
1   medium jar pimiento, diced
1   cup mayonnaise
1   (6-ounce) package wild rice mix, cooked according to directions
   bread crumbs

Sauté onions, pepper and celery until wilted, add shrimp and cook only a minute or two longer until the shrimp turn a little pink. Add all other ingredients except bread crumbs and put into 9x13-inch casserole, sprinkle crumbs on top and bake at 375 degrees for 30 minutes.

Hester Anne Kidd
Washington

Shrimp Etouffee

1	medium onion, finely chopped
2	green onions, finely chopped
3 to 4	cloves garlic, minced
1/4	cup finely chopped celery
1/2	cup butter
2	tablespoons all-purpose flour
2 1/2	cups water
1	(10 1/2-ounce) can tomato purée
2	bay leaves
1	tablespoon Worcestershire sauce
4	drops Tabasco sauce
1	tablespoon salt
1/2	teaspoon sugar
1/2	teaspoon thyme
1/8	teaspoon pepper
2	hard cooked eggs, coarsely chopped
3	cups cleaned raw shrimp (2 pounds in shell)

In large skillet, sauté onions, garlic and celery in butter until tender. Add flour; cook and stir until lightly browned. Add water, tomato purée, bay leaves, Worcestershire sauce, Tabasco sauce and seasonings. Simmer uncovered, stirring occasionally, for 25 minutes. Add shrimp and cook another 15 minutes. Garnish with eggs and serve over rice.

Yield: 6 to 8 servings

Linda Seale
Washington

Shrimp and Chicken Casserole

2	tablespoons butter
1/2	cup chopped onion
3	tablespoons all-purpose flour
	salt and pepper to taste
1 1/4	cups half and half
1/4	cup dry sherry
2	cups cooked and cut up chicken breasts
2	cups shrimp, cooked
1	can water chestnuts, sliced and drained
1	cup grated cheddar cheese
1 1/2	cups bread crumbs
	a few tablespoons of capers, if desired

Melt butter in large skillet; add onions and cook until softened. Stir in flour, salt and pepper. Add cream and sherry. Cook over medium heat stirring constantly, until mixture is smooth and somewhat thickened. Add chicken, shrimp, water chestnuts. Mix gently and pour into greased 2-quart casserole (or individual ramekins). Top with cheese and bread crumbs. Dot with butter, sprinkle with paprika and bake at 350 degrees for 35 to 45 minutes. Doubles well.

Yield: 4 servings

Hansy Jones
Washington

Shrimp and Rice Casserole

1	cup raw rice
1 1/2	pounds shrimp, cooked and cleaned
1	tablespoon lemon juice
1	tablespoon salad oil
1/4	cup minced onion
1/4	cup diced green pepper
2	tablespoons butter
1	cup heavy cream
3	tablespoons dry sherry
1	teaspoon salt
1/8	teaspoon mace
1	cup condensed tomato soup
	dash of red pepper
	dash of paprika
1/2	cup sliced almonds, lightly toasted

This can be "stretched" by adding another 1/2 pound of shrimp. Works fine.

Cook rice according to package directions. Cover shrimp with lemon juice and oil. Refrigerate until cold and crisp and stir often. Sauté onion and green pepper in butter. Drain lightly and mix with all remaining ingredients, except 1/4 cup of the almonds and paprika. Pour into 2-quart greased casserole.

Sprinkle with reserved 1/4 cup almonds and paprika. Can be made a day ahead. Cover and bake at 350 degrees for 30 minutes.

Yield: 8 to 10 servings

Mavis Rodman Peele
Washington

Baked Soft Shelled Crabs

1/2	dozen soft shelled crabs
1/2	cup cream or evaporated milk
1	egg, beaten
1	cup all-purpose flour
	salt, garlic salt and pepper to taste
	Parmesan cheese
	lemon juice

Mix flour and seasonings. Mix egg and milk. Dip crab into egg mixture, then dredge in flour mixture, and dip again in egg mixture. Heat baking dish with 1 tablespoon butter. Add crabs and bake at 500 degrees until slightly brown. Take out and sprinkle with Parmesan cheese and lemon juice. Return to oven for 5 minutes. May broil last few minutes for deeper browning.

Yield: 4 to 6 servings

Marguerite Sparrow
Washington

Soft Shell Crabs Sautéed in Brown Butter

8	soft shell crabs, cleaned and dried
2	cups milk
2	teaspoons Tabasco sauce
2	cups all-purpose flour
1	teaspoon dry mustard
1	teaspoon cayenne pepper
1	teaspoon fresh ground black pepper
1/2	teaspoon salt
6	tablespoons unsalted butter
2/3	cup fresh lemon juice, divided
1/3	cup minced parsley

Combine milk and Tabasco sauce in a shallow bowl. Combine flour, mustard, cayenne, black pepper, and salt in another bowl. Whisk to mix. Heat 2 tablespoons of butter until foaming in a large, heavy skillet over medium heat. Dip each cleaned crab in the milk mix, then dredge in the flour mix, shaking off the excess. Place crabs in the skillet (work in several batches if necessary) and sauté until done (2 to 3 minutes per side). Transfer cooked crabs to paper towels to drain, then onto a platter. Add 1/2 cup lemon juice to pan and boil over high heat until mixture is reduced to a syrupy glaze. Stir in remaining butter and cook until brown. Stir in parsley, remaining lemon juice to taste and salt and pepper to taste. Bring sauce to a boil and spoon over crabs. Serve at once.

Yield: 4 servings

Gray Murray
Washington

"Hubs Rec", a local eatery, was started in the 1940s by Hub Griffin in Belhaven. He later built on Pungo Creek and the business thrived. It was known far and wide for Hub's seafood and also his cheese biscuits. His business was destroyed by fire in 1982.

Crab Cakes

1	pound lump crabmeat, well-picked
3/4	cup crumbled saltine crackers
1	large egg
2	tablespoons minced onions
2	tablespoons mayonnaise
1	teaspoon Worcestershire sauce
1	teaspoon Dijon mustard
1	teaspoon Tabasco sauce
1	teaspoon salt

These are the best crab cakes ever…Serve with spoonbread, butter beans and sliced cucumbers in vinegar.

Mix ingredients together, reserving some cracker crumbs. Don't break up crabmeat! Form 3-inch patties. Roll in cracker crumbs. Fry in oil (1/4 inch) until brown.

Yield: 6 servings

Julie Hoell
Washington

Thora's Crab Cakes

1	pound crab meat
2	tablespoons all-purpose flour, level
2	tablespoons butter, melted
	juice 1/2 lemon
2	tablespoons mayonnaise
1	teaspoon mustard
1/2	teaspoon crab boil seasoning
	salt and pepper to taste
1	egg, beaten slightly
	cracker meal

Combine all above ingredients except egg, salt and pepper. Beat egg with salt and pepper. Form crab mixture into cakes. Roll each cake in cracker meal, dip in egg and roll again in cracker meal. Fry in hot oil.

Yield: 12 medium-sized cakes

Thora Brothers
Aurora

Grandmother Sloan's Crab Casserole

2   tablespoons margarine or butter
2   level tablespoons all-purpose flour
1   cup milk
2   eggs, hard boiled, shelled and minced
1   pound fresh crabmeat, picked over for shell pieces (clawmeat is fine)
2   slices bread, minced (remove crusts and mince, reserving crusts for top of casserole)
2   tablespoons mayonnaise
1   egg, beaten
1   tablespoon lemon juice
1   tablespoon Worcestershire sauce
      dash black pepper
      dash salt, optional
      dash Tabasco sauce, optional
1/2   teaspoon dry mustard

Make white sauce: In saucepan, add 2 tablespoons margarine or butter and allow to melt over low to medium heat. Add flour and blend well before adding milk gradually. Stir constantly until thick. Remove from heat. Add chopped hard-boiled eggs, crab, bread, mayonnaise and beaten egg to the sauce. Season with lemon juice, Worcestershire, pepper, salt, Tabasco sauce and dry mustard. Butter casserole dish. Put mixture in and top with minced bread crusts. Cheese may be sprinkled on top. Bake at 325-350 degrees for about 30 minutes.

Yield: 4 to 6 servings

Margaret Sloan Trainer
Washington

Crab and Squash Casserole

2	pounds (6 cups) squash
1/4	cup chopped onion

Cook for 5 to 10 minutes in a little water and drain.

Combine and add to the above:

1	can cream of chicken soup
1	cup sour cream
1	pound crabmeat (check for shells)

Blend:

1/2	cup melted margarine or butter
1	(8-ounce) package corn meal stuffing mix, divided

Spread part of stuffing in the bottom of a greased 2-quart baking dish. Then add squash/crab mixture; add remaining stuffing and bake at 350 degrees for about 40 minutes.

Yield: 8 servings

Lillian V. Hooker
Aurora

Crabmeat and Asparagus

1	pound crabmeat
2	tablespoons butter
1/2	cup dry sherry
2	tablespoons all-purpose flour
2	cups light cream
	salt and pepper
2	(10-ounce) packages frozen asparagus
1	cup whipping cream, whipped
4	tablespoons grated Parmesan cheese

Sauté crab lightly in butter. Add sherry and simmer until reduced by one-half. Add flour and then cream, stirring constantly until thickened. Add seasonings. Fork stir, keeping crab in lumps. Cook and drain asparagus. Place asparagus in bottom of a buttered casserole. Pour crab mixture over asparagus. Spread with whipped cream. Sprinkle with cheese and brown under low heat. (You may use 2 cans of asparagus.)

Gloria Fentress
Washington

Many Washington residents remember the Knotty Pine Inn. Here's a sample of the 1975 menu.

Crab Cakes	*$1.60*
Fried Oysters	*2.75*
Shad Roe and Bacon	*2.50*
Fried Chicken (1/4)	*1.50*

Prices include tossed salad, baked potato, rolls, coffee or tea

James M. Harrell, Jr. opened Knotty Pine Inn June 5, 1945, on Hackney Avenue in Washington. He had a garden and in the summer he would serve his fresh vegetables, including corn, string beans, squash and butter beans.

Deviled Crab

1	pound crabmeat, well-picked
1/2	cup evaporated milk
1/2	cup butter
	salt and cayenne pepper to taste
	juice of 2 lemons
1	teaspoon mustard
2	hard boiled eggs, mashed fine
1/2	cup biscuit or cracker crumbs
	crab shells, cleaned

Mix all ingredients, place in shells and sprinkle with buttered crumbs. Place in oven and cook at 350 degrees until very hot.

Ellen Morgan
by her daughter-in-law, Gayle Morgan
Washington

The Belhaven Crab Festival is held during the summer. Activities include crab dish(es) tasting, crab races, arts and crafts, and varied entertainment.

Crabmeat Casserole

1	pound lump crabmeat, picked through for shell
1	cup chopped celery
1/2	cup chopped onions
1	cup mayonnaise
1	lemon, juiced
2	cups seasoned croutons
1	dash Tabasco sauce
	salt
	pepper
1/2	cup fine dry bread crumbs
1/2	cup Parmesan cheese
1/2	stick butter

Combine everything except bread crumbs, butter and cheese. Put mix in a greased 2-quart casserole dish. Sprinkle with remaining ingredients. Bake at 350 degrees for 1 hour.

Yield: 8 servings

Betty Tubaugh
Washington

This recipe is from The River Forest Manor in Belhaven, NC. It is easy and very good.

The River Forest Manor, on the Pungo in Belhaven, was originally a Victorian mansion built in 1899 by John A. Wilkerson at a cost of around $53,000. It is the focal point for overnight stops by yachts using the Intracoastal Waterway. It is known for its delicious buffets. Many people looked forward to the Sunday buffet after church. In 1981, the "Sequoia" docked at the River Forest Manor. This yacht served 8 presidents!

Sea Island Supper

2	cups cooked white rice
6 to 8	ounces crabmeat
1	cup good mayonnaise
1/8	teaspoon pepper
1/2	cup minced green pepper
1/2	cup minced onions
1	can water chestnuts, thinly sliced
1 1/2	pounds shelled, cooked shrimp
	cheese or bread crumbs

Mix all ingredients together lightly and fill a greased 3-quart casserole. When ready to cook, sprinkle cheese or crumbs on top. Bake at 350 degrees for 25 minutes.

Yield: 8 to 10 servings

Mildred Rumley
Washington

Oyster Casserole

The oyster has always been a prized food item. This unusual animal begins life as a female and becomes a male later! It spawns during the months without an "R". Before the invention of the freezer, oysters were never eaten during warm weather.

3	dozen raw oysters, or 12 ounces select oysters, or enough to make 1 1/2 cups oysters, drained with juice reserved
3	cups coarsely rolled crackers (unsalted wafers), divided
1/4	cup oyster juice
1 1/2	cups milk or half and half
1	teaspoon salt (optional)
2	eggs, slightly beaten
	pinch of pepper (optional)

Prepare cracker crumbs. Arrange 1/4 crumbs in bottom of greased 2-quart casserole; put 12 oysters over crackers; alternate crackers and oysters, finishing with cracker crumbs on top. Scald oyster juice, milk and butter together. Add salt and pepper and combine with beaten eggs. Pour mixture over crackers and oysters. (2 tablespoon minced onion may be used on top if desired.) Bake at 350 degrees for one hour.

Marion Leiner
Washington

Tar Heel Oysters

4 to 8 tablespoons butter
2 dozen or so raw oysters
　　　salt, pepper and nutmeg to taste
4 slices very hard, buttered toast

Simmer oysters in butter until lips curl. Season with salt, pepper and nutmeg and serve immediately on hard buttered toast. Simply delicious if served hot, but dreadful if you poke around until they are cold!

A spinach soufflé and a watercress salad go nicely with these Eastern Carolina treats.

Yield: 4 servings (approximately)

Betsy Robbins
Washington

Fried Oysters

1 pint oysters, drained
2 eggs, beaten with a little salt, pepper and 1 tablespoon vinegar
1/2 roll of saltines, rolled medium fine

Dip oysters in egg mixture and then in crumbs. Fry on hot griddle or skillet. Remove when brown and drain on brown paper.

Mildred Rumley
Washington

It may be an old wives tale, but some say its best to avoid sweets after eating oysters.

In the early 1900s, people went down to the docks and bought oysters in the shell. Many folks would take their own vinegar and crackers and eat as many oysters as they wanted for 5 cents a piece.

Oyster roasts on the Pamlico were and continue to be a popular "dining experience." Crowds of up to one hundred will be invited to stand around tables and open their own oysters. Bring your own oyster knife!

Baked Flounder, Ocracoke style

1	cup water
6	medium potatoes, peeled and sliced 1/4-inch thick
2	pounds flounder filets, cut into 4-inch pieces
1	large onion, cut into 1/4-inch slices and separated into rings
	salt and pepper to taste
1/2	cup chopped green onion
1/4	cup coarsely chopped salt pork

Pour water in a greased 9x13-inch baking pan. Layer 1/3 of potatoes, flounder and onion rings in pan. Sprinkle with salt, pepper and 1/3 of green onions. Repeat layers twice. Sprinkle with salt pork. Cover with foil and bake at 350 degrees for 1 hour. Uncover and bake until potatoes are tender, about 30 minutes.

Yield: 4 to 6 servings

Irene Forbes
Washington

Seafood Lasagna

2	tablespoons olive oil, divided
1	(8-ounce) box lasagna noodles
1 1/2	pound medium size shrimp, shelled, deveined and cut into small pieces
1 1/2	pound medium size scallops, cleaned and sliced into small pieces
1/4	teaspoon oregano
	dash of pepper
3	eggs, beaten
2	(16-ounce) cans spaghetti sauce (chunky garden or flavor of your choice)
1	pint ricotta cheese
2	(8-ounce) bags shredded mozzarella cheese
2	tablespoons Parmesan cheese

In a pot of boiling water, add 1 tablespoon oil and the lasagna noodles and boil until tender (approximately 10 to 15 minutes) then set aside. Heat remaining tablespoon olive oil in pan and sauté shrimp and scallops and a dash of pepper (about 1 minute). Add spaghetti sauce and 1/4 teaspoon oregano and let simmer for about 5 minutes. Preheat oven to 350 degrees. In a bowl, mix all the cheeses and the beaten eggs. In an oven-proof glass 10x15-inch baking dish or aluminum foil pan, spray with vegetable cooking spray, layer 1/3 of the spaghetti sauce mixture, noodles (drained), cheese mixture, then sauce, and a layer of noodles; top off with sauce. Bake for about 30 to 40 minutes.

Yield: 6 to 8 servings

Audrey Whitley
Washington

Fried Herring

This recipe works well for any small fish such as pan trout or white perch. Allow 1/3 to 1/2 pound per person.

Purchase dressed herring with heads removed. Wash and let drain. Using sharp knife, make gashes in fish about 1/2-inch apart on both sides from head to tail. Generously season a pan of cornmeal with salt and black pepper. Roll fish in this mixture, then shake off excess. Have ready a heavy, deep pan about half full of peanut oil heated to 375 degrees. Place fish into hot oil, and cook until crisp and brown. Fish will rise to the top when done. This takes about 3 to 5 minutes. Serve hot.

Tranters Creek Herring Club
Washington

Three Cheese Chicken Bake

8	ounces noodles
2	tablespoons butter
1/4	cup chopped onion
1/2	cup chopped green pepper
1	can cream of chicken soup
1/3	cup milk
1	(6-ounce) can mushrooms, drained
1/4	cup chopped pimiento
1	cup creamed cottage cheese
3	cups chicken, cooked and diced
2	cups American cheese, shredded
1/2	cup grated Parmesan cheese

Cook noodles until tender. Drain and rinse in cold water. For sauce, sauté onion and pepper in butter. Stir in soup, add milk, mushrooms and pimiento. Arrange half of noodles in baking dish; cover with half each of the sauce, cottage cheese, chicken and other cheeses. Repeat layers and bake at 350 degrees for 45 minutes.

Yield: 4 to 6 servings

Roy Tucker
Chocowinity

Chicken with Walnuts

A family favorite from the Peking school. The peppers are sweet and the taste is fantastic. One of my favorites and low calorie too. Serve over brown rice.

1	cup walnut halves
2	whole chicken breasts, skinned, boned and cut into 1/2-inch cubes
2	bell peppers, one red and one green cut into 1/2-inch cubes
2	tablespoons bean sauce
2	tablespoons sugar
1/4	cup chicken stock
1	tablespoon dry sherry
3	tablespoons oil, divided

Toast walnuts in 350 degree oven until brown (5 to 10 minutes). Stir-fry chicken in 1 tablespoon oil and remove. Stir-fry peppers 1 minute and remove. Cook bean sauce in 1 tablespoon oil 3 minutes; lower heat. Add sugar and stir 30 seconds before adding chicken stock and sherry. Stir until dark brown. Turn up heat. Pour in chicken and peppers. Stir-fry quickly for 1 minute before removing to platter. Sprinkle walnuts over chicken.

Shirley Padgett
Chocowinity

Lemon Mustard Chicken

6	skinned chicken breasts
1/2	stick butter
3	tablespoons Dijon mustard
3	tablespoons fresh lemon juice
1	teaspoon tarragon
	pinch of salt

Preheat oven to 375 degrees. Place chicken in shallow pan. Melt butter, stir in mustard, lemon juice, tarragon and salt. Pour over chicken and bake for 45 minutes to 1 hour, uncovered. Check after 30 minutes; it may be done if chicken is thin.

Yield: 6 servings

Helen Sommerkamp
Aurora

Fried chicken was never served in the winter in the early 1900s. You served fried chicken in the spring when "Spring Chickens" were available.

Pot-Roasted Chicken with Artichokes

An excellent 'fancy' dish that tastes out-of-this-world, yet is surprisingly simple to make. I always get more compliments for this than some of the more difficult dishes I tackle.

12	small, white onions, peeled (about 3/4 pound)
2	tablespoons olive oil
2	tablespoons butter
1	whole chicken, 3 to 4 pounds
8 to 10	small, red potatoes scrubbed
	or, though not as good, 2 cups diced potatoes
1	package frozen artichoke hearts, quartered
1/2	pound mushrooms, quartered if large
1	(10-ounce) package frozen snow peas
	salt and pepper
1/2	teaspoon thyme
1/2	teaspoon marjoram
1/2	cup dry white wine
1/2	cup chicken bouillon or stock

Heat butter and oil in a large, heavy skillet; add onions and brown lightly. Remove onions. Brown the chicken on all sides, then place it in a casserole. Arrange the onions, potatoes, artichoke hearts, mushrooms and pea pods around the chicken. Add the herbs, salt and pepper, wine and stock. Bake covered at 350 degrees 1 1/2 hours, or until chicken is very tender. Bring to the table in a casserole. Remove chicken to a warm platter to carve. Serve the vegetables from the casserole.

Yield: 4 servings

Nancy H. Nash
Washington

Lemon Chicken with Thyme

3	tablespoons all-purpose flour
1/2	teaspoon salt
1/4	teaspoon pepper
4	skinless, boneless chicken breast halves
2	tablespoons olive oil
1	medium onion
1	tablespoon margarine
1	cup chicken broth
3	tablespoons lemon juice
1/2	teaspoon thyme
	lemon wedges (optional)
2	tablespoons chopped parsley (optional)

In a plastic or paper bag, combine flour, salt and pepper and shake to mix. Add the chicken and shake to coat lightly. Remove the chicken and reserve the excess seasoned flour. In a large skillet, warm 1 tablespoon of the oil over medium heat. Add the chicken and brown on one side, 5 minutes. Add the remaining 1 table-spoon oil, turn chicken and brown well on the second side, about 5 minutes longer. Transfer chicken to a plate and set aside.

Coarsely chop the onion. Add the margarine to the skillet and cook onion for 2 to 3 minutes. Stir in the reserved seasoned flour and cook, stirring until the flour is completely incorporated, about 1 minute. Add the broth, 2 tablespoons of the lemon juice, and the thyme and bring mixture to a boil, stirring constantly. Return the chicken to the skillet, reduce heat to medium low and cover. Cook until chicken is tender and opaque throughout, about 25 minutes. Remove chicken, stir in the remaining 1 tablespoon lemon juice in the skillet and pour over chicken. Serve with lemon wedges and parsley.

Yield: 4 servings

Sadie Fowle
Washington

The Patrician Inn was a well-known inn owned and operated by Mr. and Mrs. David Pickles. This elegant house was filled with priceless antiques and silver which was used in serving lunch and dinner. It was located on East Main Street in Washington in an area which is now a parking lot.

Sherried Chicken Breasts

12	boned chicken breast halves
12	slices Swiss cheese
2	(10-ounce) cans cream of chicken soup
1	cup dry sherry
1 1/2	cups dry herb stuffing mix
1/2	cup margarine, melted

Place chicken breasts in a well-greased 9x13-inch baking dish. Place cheese slices over the chicken. Mix soup and sherry and pour over chicken. Sprinkle stuffing mix on top and drizzle melted margarine over the top. Bake uncovered at 300 degrees for 1 1/2 hours or until chicken is done.

Yield: 12 servings

Alice McClure
Washington

Chicken Paprika

1	(3 to 4-pound) fryer
	salt and pepper to taste
2	tablespoons butter
2	tablespoons oil
5	tablespoons all-purpose flour
2	cups water
1	cup sour cream
1 to 2	teaspoons paprika (more if desired)
1/2	cup dry sherry (or more if desired)

Dust serving size pieces of chicken with salt and pepper. Heat butter and oil in large, heavy skillet; add chicken and sauté until golden brown, turning frequently. Remove chicken from pan and add flour to drippings, blend well; add water, sour cream and paprika; cook, stirring constantly until thick and smooth. Return chicken to pan and cover tightly. Simmer for 45 minutes to an hour or until tender. Arrange chicken on a plate. Add sherry to gravy, season with salt and pepper, and serve over chicken.

Yield: 4 servings

Terry Knott
Washington

Deep Dish Cheddar Chicken

1/2	stick butter
1/2	cup chopped onion
1/4	cup all-purpose flour
3/4	teaspoon sage
1/4	cup milk
2	large chicken breasts, cooked and cubed with broth reserved
1	cup chicken broth (from reserved broth)
10	ounces cooked broccoli, cut into bite size pieces
8	ounces cheddar cheese, grated
1	can refrigerated crescent rolls

Fresh or frozen broccoli, lightly cooked, may be used.

Sauté onion in butter. Mix in dry ingredients and add milk and broth slowly, stirring constantly until mixture is thick. Remove from heat, put chopped chicken, broccoli and cheese in greased 9x13-inch dish and pour sauce over all. Pat out crescent rolls and put over the chicken mixture in any design you may wish, cupping the ends around edge of dish to form a lip. Bake at 350 degrees for 25 to 30 minutes or until roll dough is lightly browned.

Yield: 8 to 10 servings

Lorrie Beach
Washington

Buttermilk Pecan Chicken

1/3	cup butter
1	cup all-purpose flour
1/4	cup sesame seeds
1	teaspoon paprika
1 1/2	teaspoons salt
1/8	teaspoon pepper
1	cup ground pecans
1	egg, beaten
1	cup buttermilk
8	chicken breasts, skinned and boned
1/4	cup coarsely chopped pecans

Melt butter in a 9x13-inch baking dish. Set aside. Combine next 6 ingredients to make seasoned flour mixture. Combine egg and buttermilk. Dip chicken in egg mixture and dredge in flour mixture, coating well. Place chicken in baking dish, turning once to coat in butter. Sprinkle with chopped pecans. Bake at 350 degrees for 30 minutes or until done.

Yield: 8 servings

Ruth Hopkins
Washington

Chicken Monterey

8	boneless chicken breast halves
1/2	teaspoon salt
1/4	teaspoon pepper
1/2	cup all-purpose flour
1/2	cup butter, divided
1/2	cup chopped onion
1	clove garlic, minced
8 to 10	mushrooms, chopped
2	tablespoons all-purpose flour
1	teaspoon celery salt
1/2	teaspoon white pepper
1/2	cup chicken stock (or broth)
1/2	cup white wine
1	avocado, mashed
6	ounces Monterey Jack cheese, grated

Pound chicken to 1/4 inch thickness. Mix together flour, pepper and salt. Lightly sprinkle chicken with flour mixture, sauté quickly in 1/4 cup butter. Place in 3-quart baking dish. In same skillet and remaining butter. Sauté onion, garlic and mushrooms until tender. Stir in seasonings, flour, broth and wine. Cook over low heat until thickened (4 to 5 minutes). Stir in avocado and 1/2 cup cheese. Blend well. Pour mixture over chicken. Top with remaining cheese.

Bake at 350 degrees for 15 minutes if serving immediately. To make ahead, refrigerate covered. Warm to room temperature and bake at 350 degrees for 25 to 30 minutes.

Yield: 8 servings

Nancy Collis
Washington

Tetrazzini

1	large chicken, cut up
1	pound bacon, cooked until crisp
4	medium onions, chopped
1	(26-ounce) can diced tomatoes
1	large jar sliced mushrooms
1	(10-ounce) package extra sharp cheddar cheese, divided
1	(16-ounce) package thin spaghetti
	salt and pepper to taste

In large pot, heat water to boil, add chicken. When water returns to boil, turn heat down to simmer and cook for 40 minutes. Cool in stock, reserving stock. When chicken is cool, remove and discard skin, fat and bones and cut meat into bite-sized pieces. Cook bacon in oven, crumble, and pour off almost all of the fat.

Sauté onions in remaining bacon grease until clear. Add tomatoes and simmer about 1/2 hour. Add chicken, bacon, drained mushrooms, and 1/2 of cheese, cubed to tomato-onion mixture. DO NOT COOK.

Break spaghetti into bite-sized pieces and cook according to directions on box, using the chicken stock and more water, if needed, for the cooking liquid. Drain, add tomato mixture, salt and pepper to taste. Pour into greased 9x12-inch casserole, cover with foil and bake at 350 degrees for 1/2 hour or until hot. Just before removing from oven, remove foil and cover with remainder of cheese, grated. May be made ahead and also may be frozen.

Yield: 12 servings

Laura Bell
Washington

Chicken Spaghetti Casserole

3	tablespoons margarine or butter
3	tablespoons all-purpose flour
1	teaspoon salt
1/8	teaspoon pepper
1	teaspoon dry mustard
2/3	cup chicken broth
1/2	pound grated cheddar cheese
6	cooked chicken breasts, cut into bite size pieces
1	teaspoon Worcestershire sauce
1	(14 1/2-ounce) can tomatoes (if large pieces, cut smaller)
1	can cream of mushroom soup
3	cups cooked spaghetti, or more if desired

In large pan or pot, melt margarine or butter. Blend in flour, salt, mustard, pepper and cook I minutè on low heat. Add tomatoes, then cheese, stirring constantly until cheese is melted. Add soup, broth, Worcestershire sauce and blend. Add chicken and spaghetti. Turn into lightly-greased large casserole. If desired, sprinkle with additional cheese. Bake at 375 degrees for 35 minutes.

Yield: 8 to 10 servings

Ethel Schramm
Chocowinity

Special Chicken Casserole

3	cups cooked chicken
1	(6-ounce) package cooked long grain and wild rice mix
1	medium onion, chopped
1	can cream of celery soup
1	cup mayonnaise
1	can water chestnuts, sliced and drained
2	cans French-sliced green beans, drained
1/2	cup chopped red bell pepper or pimiento

Mix all ingredients and add salt and pepper to taste. Pour into a lightly-greased 3-quart baking dish. Bake at 350 degrees for 25 to 30 minutes. May be frozen before baking. Bring to room temperature and bake as above.

Yield: 8 to 10 servings

Mildred Buckman
Washington

In 1946, Lib and Raymond Latham opened "The Rendezvous" near the corner of John Small Avenue and Ninth Street in Washington. Originally planned as a sandwich shop, the place quickly developed into a complete restaurant. A good meal could be purchased for 75 cents at this time. With good food, a homey, friendly atmosphere and congenial hosts, The Rendezvous was a very popular place. The Lathams sold their business in 1974.

Hot Chicken Salad with Pecan Topping

3	cups cooked, chopped chicken breasts
1	(8-ounce) can sliced water chestnuts
3/4	cup mayonnaise
1 1/2	cup chopped celery
1	can cream of mushroom soup
	salt and pepper to taste
1	stick butter
1/2	(8-ounce) package of herb-seasoned stuffing mix
1	cup of pecan halves, buttered and toasted

I have a friend who collects chicken recipes, and she says this is the BEST she has ever tasted.

Mix together first 6 ingredients. Spoon into well-buttered 1 1/2-quart casserole dish. Melt butter, mix with stuffing mix. Sprinkle over top of casserole. Layer pecan halves on top of dressing.

Bake at 350 degrees for about 30 minutes (until bubbly).

Yield: 8 servings

Lib Ross
Washington

Rice-Stuffed Cornish Hens

2	Cornish hens
1	(6-ounce) package long grain and wild rice mix, cooked according to directions
	melted butter
1	small jar currant jelly
1	teaspoon orange liqueur
1	teaspoon lemon-lime liqueur
1	small can frozen orange juice concentrate

Salt and pepper hens inside and out. Stuff with cooked rice. Brush with melted butter. Bake at 350 degrees for 1/2 hour. Combine jelly, liqueurs and orange juice. Spread over hens. Bake an additional 40 minutes, basting with sauce. Serve with sauce around each hen.

Yield: 2 servings or 4 servings if you split the hens and serve as part of a large meal.

Hester Anne Kidd
Washington

Stuffed Hens in Salt Clay

Allow one bird per person.

6   **(12 to 16-ounce) Cornish hens**
1   **tablespoon salt and 1 teaspoon pepper, mixed**
1/4   **cup cooking oil**

Wash hens; dry well; fold wings; tie legs together. Sprinkle each bird with a little of the salt and pepper mixture. Brush each with a little of the oil. Wrap each bird completely in one layer of foil; pressing tightly against body to eliminate air pockets. Proceed with wrapping each bird with salt clay.

Salt Clay

(makes one batch - enough for one bird)

1 1/4   **cup regular table salt**
1   **cup unsifted, all-purpose flour**
1/2   **cup water**

Mix flour and salt together in bowl. Add the water and quickly mix to form a loose ball. Place clay ball on well floured board and knead until smooth - only a few minutes. Roll out to a 9x10 inch square. Set foil-wrapped bird in center, bringing clay up around bird to seal completely. Cut decorative shapes from excess clay; moisten surface and apply to outside, pressing to adhere. Bake at 475 degrees for 1 1/2 hours. Cover top with foil last 30 minutes to prevent over browning. Let cool 10 to 15 minutes before serving.

To serve, place bird on each dinner plate. Provide small brass (or other hard material) hammer to break open clay coat. Use extra napkin to cover clay to prevent spatter when clay is broken open. Also provide small plate to receive broken clay pieces and foil.

Clay sets very quickly, so do only one bird and batch at the time. Birds may be done ahead (even over night) if they are carefully refrigerated. This is fun to do and not as complicated as it sounds.

Yield: 6 servings

Louise Lane
Washington

A "smashingly" different entrée for very special dinner parties.

Fried Turkey

1	(12 to 15-pound) turkey
	salt
	cayenne pepper
3 ½ to 4	gallons peanut oil

Rinse turkey and pat dry inside and out. Sprinkle with salt and cayenne. Pour enough oil to cover turkey in 40 quart pot. Turkey must be completely covered. Make sure pot is large enough that oil won't overflow. Heat oil to 350 to 375 degrees. Holding legs, SLOWLY and CAREFULLY lower bird in oil. Be careful not to splash any oil. Fry bird 3 to 4 minutes per pound (a 15 pound bird will be done in 50 to 60 minutes). Tongs or a large fork make handling easier. Test for doneness at bone at thigh joint. Carefully remove turkey from oil. Allow to drain.

Yield: 10 to 12 servings, perhaps with leftovers

Tucker Talley
Washington

Hot Browns

This recipe is named after a dish created in the kitchens of the famous Brown Hotel in Louisville, Kentucky. It is a delicious way to use leftover turkey from the holiday celebrations. For a crowd, the hot browns can be assembled on a cookie sheet.

4	slices toasted white bread
8 to 12	thin slices turkey breast
1	bunch fresh broccoli, slightly undercooked
4	thick slices of fresh tomato (optional)
4	slices partially cooked bacon
	cheese sauce

Place one piece of toast in an individual ramekin. Cover with two or more slices of turkey. Place several florets of cooked broccoli on top of turkey and cover with a thick tomato slice. Generously cover with cheese sauce and top with partially cooked bacon. Run ramekins under a preheated broiler for about 10 minutes, until bacon is cooked and the cheese sauce is slightly brown.

Cheese Sauce

2	tablespoons margarine or butter
2	tablespoons all-purpose flour
1 1/2	cups milk
	salt and cayenne pepper, to taste
2	teaspoons grated onion
1 to 2	cups grated cheddar cheese

Melt butter in small saucepan. Stir in flour with a large fork until mixture forms a smooth paste. Add milk slowly and stir over medium heat until smooth. Add salt, cayenne pepper, grated onion, and cheddar cheese, stirring until cheese is melted.

Sue Nicholson
Bath

Turkey Pie with Sage Pastry

1/2   cup butter
1/2   cup all-purpose flour
1 1/8 teaspoons salt
1/4   teaspoon ground sage
1/8   teaspoon pepper
1/8   teaspoon mace
1   teaspoon lemon juice
1 1/2 cups turkey broth
1   cup milk
3   cups turkey, cooked and diced
      sage pastry

Melt butter and blend in flour and seasonings. Add lemon juice, broth and milk. Cook, stirring until thickened. Add turkey and heat. Pour into quart casserole, which has been sprayed with vegetable cooking spray. Cover with sage pastry. Cut gashes in top of pastry to vent. Bake at 425 degrees for 20 minutes.

Sage Pastry

1/2   cup all-purpose flour
1/2   teaspoon salt
3   tablespoons water
1/2   teaspoon sage
1/2   cup cornmeal
1/3   cup butter

Combine dry ingredients, cut in butter, add water and roll crust to fit over casserole.

Yield: 4 servings

Sage pastry may be patted out by hand to fit casserole, an easier process than rolling.

*Irene Forbes
Washington*

Lemon Glazed Pork Chops

The ritual of hog killing is almost a lost art, but a few families still practice it. Originally a two-day project, today ready-to-process hogs are purchased. At dawn on a cold winter's day, work begins with the help of friends and neighbors. Hams are cut for curing, pieces of meat are cut and ground for sausage, and cuts are prepared for roasts and chops. The fat is put into a big iron pot to render for lard. Already the air is filled with the aroma of a thick, rich hog stew. The host family provides the midday meal, and tables are loaded with turkey, ham, and many vegetables, salads and desserts. At noon, others arrive, bringing more food. By this time, as many as 30 items are ready to be consumed. This is an unforgettable experience, so don't pass it up!

The families of Steve Douglas, the Black brothers, and Phil Garris

4 to 6 pork chops
1 tablespoon all-purpose flour
1/2 teaspoon salt
1/4 teaspoon pepper
2 tablespoons oil
1 tablespoon soy sauce
1/4 cup brown sugar
2 teaspoons cornstarch
1/4 cup white vinegar
1/4 cup honey
3 tablespoons lemon juice
1/2 cup chopped onions

In plastic bag, shake chops and flour, salt and pepper. Brown on both sides. Pour off excess grease. In a small bowl, combine all other ingredients except onion. Pour over the chops, sprinkle onions over all, cover and simmer 15 to 20 minutes. If it thickens too much during cooking, add a little water.

Yield: 4 to 6 servings

Leah Pyburn
Washington

Pork Chop Casserole

4 1-inch thick pork chops
2 tablespoons melted shortening
1 1/2 cups uncooked regular rice
1 (16-ounce) can tomato wedges, undrained
1 (10 1/2-ounce) can beef consommé
1 package dried onion soup mix
1 teaspoon thyme
1 teaspoon oregano
salt and pepper to taste

Brown chops in shortening. Spray vegetable cooking spray in shallow 2-quart casserole dish. Pour in rice. Lay chops on top. Combine tomatoes, consommé, onion soup mix, thyme, oregano, salt and pepper. Pour over chops. Cover and bake at 350 degrees for 1 hour and 15 minutes.

Yield: 4 servings

Jean Duke Trueblood
Washington

Farmer's Pork Chops

8	medium potatoes
8	center cut pork chops
1	large onion, cut into 8 slices
1	cup all-purpose flour
2	tablespoons seasoning salt
1/3	cup oil

White Sauce

1	stick butter
1/2	cup all-purpose flour
1 to 2	teaspoons salt
1/2 to 3/4	teaspoon black pepper
1/4	cup chopped parsley or chives
4	cups milk

Melt butter, remove from heat, stir in flour, salt and pepper. Return to heat, stirring constantly until mixture is bubbly. Add milk, 1 cup at a time, bring to boil over medium heat and simmer 1 to 2 minutes. Add parsley or chives and let stand for a few minutes.

Preheat oven to 350 degrees. Peel and slice potatoes, 1/4 inch thick. Cover with cold water. Slice onion thinly. Drain potatoes and layer 1/2 of them in greased 9x12-inch dish. Sprinkle with salt and pepper. Scatter 1/2 onion over potatoes and cover with 1/2 of the white sauce. Repeat this process with other 1/2 of potatoes, onion and white sauce. Cover dish with plastic wrap and microwave 5 minutes on high or bake, uncovered, for 15 minutes.

Mix flour and seasoning salt and dredge pork chops. Lightly brown on both sides. As chops are removed from frying pan, place them on top of potatoes. Bake at 350 degrees for 45 to 60 minutes.

Yield: 8 servings

Alva Douglas
Douglas Crossroads

Pork Loin in Style

3 to 4 pounds pork loin roast
1 tablespoon shortening
salt
pepper
1/2 cup water
1 (8-ounce) can tomato sauce
1 (16-ounce) can sauerkraut
1 small head cabbage

This delicious main course is complete when served with boiled potatoes or buttered egg noodles.

Brown the roast on all sides, using a Dutch oven and the tablespoon of shortening. Season with salt and pepper, add the 1/2 cup water, cover and cook over low to medium heat for 2 hours, or more if you desire.

Cut cabbage as if making coarse cole slaw and layer the sauerkraut, cabbage, and tomato sauce around the roast in the Dutch oven. Repeat with a second layer. Rinse the tomato sauce can with a small amount of water and pour that in also. Cook covered for 30 more minutes on low heat.

Carefully stir and cook 30 minutes longer. (You may increase your total cooking time according to the size of your roast and how well-done you prefer your food.)

Yield: 8 servings

Dolores M. Tate
Belhaven

Pork Piccata

2	pork tenderloins (3/4 pound each)
1/2	cup all-purpose flour
1/2	teaspoon salt
1/4	teaspoon pepper
3	tablespoons olive oil
1/2	cup white wine
1/2	cup lemon juice (fresh)
3	tablespoons margarine or butter
1/4	cup chopped fresh parsley
1 1/2	tablespoons capers

Cut each tenderloin into 6 (2-ounce) medallions. Place medallions between heavy duty plastic wrap and flatten with mallet to 1/4 inch thickness. Combine flour, salt and pepper and dredge pork. Cook half of the pork medallions in 1 1/2 tablespoons of oil over medium heat for 2 minutes a side or until lightly browned. Remove and keep warm while you repeat with other half pork medallions. Add wine and lemon juice to the skillet and heat thoroughly. Add butter, parsley and capers, stirring until butter melts. Add pork and heat through. Serve over fettucini or pasta of choice. Garnish with thin slices of lemon and parsley.

Yield: 6 servings

Linda Seale
Washington

A pig pickin' continues to be one of Beaufort County's favorite ways of entertaining a crowd. The ingredients are few; the pig, a large grill, someone with the skill and time for long, slow cooking, a vinegar-base sauce (the hotter the better), slaw and stewed potatoes, fried lace cornbread and hushpuppies, too. Get there early if you want to get your share of the ribs!

Cold Buffet Pork

3 to 5 pounds boneless pork loin
2 small carrots
2 stalks of celery
1 medium onion, stuck with 4 whole cloves

This is my variation of the Italian dish "Vitello Tonnato." It makes a delicious and beautiful addition to a buffet presentation.

Put meat into saucepan large enough to hold the pork; fill pan with water to cover. Remove pork and set aside. Add other ingredients and bring water to boil. When it is at a low boil, put the pork back in, reduce the heat, and cover. Keep at a slow simmer for at least 2 hours. Turn off heat and leave meat in water until cool.

Sauce

1 (7-ounce) can of tuna
4 anchovy fillets
1 cup of olive oil
2 1/2 tablespoons of lemon juice
3 tablespoons of small capers, drained
1 1/2 cups homemade mayonnaise

Blend the above until well mixed and fold into 1 1/2 cups of homemade mayonnaise.

When the meat is cold and firm, cut it into thin slices. Spread a serving platter with some of the sauce, cover with some slices of pork, then spread on the sauce and more meat. The pork should be completely covered with the sauce. Repeat until pork and sauce are completely used up. Cover with plastic wrap and refrigerate for at least 24 hours. Garnish as desired before serving.

Joan Conlon
Washington

Hap's Cold Pork Tenderloin

3	pounds pork tenderloins
2/3	cup soy sauce
2/3	cup brown sugar
1	tablespoon cornstarch
2	tablespoons vinegar
2	teaspoons ground ginger
3	cloves garlic, minced
2/3	cup finely chopped candied or crystallized ginger

Place tenderloins in 9x13-inch glass baking dish or large zip-top plastic bags. Combine all ingredients except candied ginger and pour over meat. Marinate 6 to 8 hours or overnight. Bake in preheated 350 degree oven 30 to 45 minutes per pound. Remove meat from pan when done and let cool. Save sauce. Slice meat into 1/4 inch slices and arrange in small dish or plate with sides. Add reserved ginger to sauce and pour over meat. Refrigerate 4 to 6 hours before serving.

Yield: 10 to 12 servings

Katirie Leach
Washington

Marinated Pork Tenderloin

2	3/4 to 1 pound tenderloins

Marinade

1/4	cup honey
1/4	cup soy sauce
2	tablespoons brown sugar
1	tablespoon ginger
1	tablespoon minced garlic
1	tablespoon ketchup
1/2	teaspoon onion powder

Mix and pour over tenderloins. Marinate 8 hours or overnight. Grill 30 minutes or bake at 350 degrees until meat thermometer registers done for pork.

Yield: 6 to 8 servings

Peggy Hudson
Washington

Barbecued Pork Tenderloin

1/2   cup pork dry rub (see below)
2   (1 1/4-pound) pork tenderloins
1   cup honey pork sauce (see below)

Cover pork on all sides with rub and refrigerate 8 hours, turning occasionally. Cook on grill, turning as needed to prevent meat from becoming too brown. Meat should reach 160 degrees when done.

Baste with Honey Sauce during the last 5 minutes or so.

Pork Dry Rub

1/4   cup paprika
2   tablespoons dried thyme
2   tablespoons dried rosemary
2   tablespoons garlic powder
1/2   teaspoon ground black pepper
1/4   teaspoon cayenne pepper

In small bowl, combine all and mix well. Rub the mixture on all sides of pork and refrigerate,

Honey Pork Sauce

1   cup ketchup
1/2   cup honey
1/4   cup Madeira or other sweet wine
2   tablespoons cider vinegar
12   teaspoons Worcestershire sauce

Mix well.

Yield: 8 to 10 servings

Nannette Smyre
Chocowinity

A typical "dination", as big dinners were called, included a six-week-old suckling pig, roasted with a red apple in its mouth, a roast at one end of the table and a boiled turkey with egg dressing at the other end.

Oriental Pork Tenderloin

1 1/2 to 2 **pounds pork tenderloin**
1/4 **cup soy sauce**
1/4 **cup cider vinegar**
2 **tablespoons dark brown sugar**
2 **tablespoons honey**
2/3 **cup apricot preserves**
1 1/2 **tablespoons Dijon mustard**

Rinse meat and pat dry. Mix next four ingredients and pour over meat in dish. Cover with plastic wrap and marinate overnight. Turn several times. Preheat oven to 350 degrees. Pour off marinade and reserve. Spoon 1/4 cup marinade over meat and bake 30 to 40 minutes, or until fork tender. Baste every 10 minutes with an additional tablespoonful of reserved marinade. Combine apricot preserves and mustard. Spoon over meat and bake an additional 10 minutes. Slice into thin slices and top with pan glaze.

Yield: 6 to 8 servings

Phyllis Encinias
Chocowinity

Country Ham with Red-eye Gravy

3 **slices country ham (about 1/2-inch thick)**
1/4 **cup butter**
1/4 **cup brown sugar, firmly packed**
1 **cup strong brewed coffee**

Cut most of the fat from ham slices; melt butter in heavy skillet and cook ham 5 minutes on each side until browned. Remove ham from skillet and keep ham warm. Stir brown sugar into hot drippings until dissolved. Add coffee, bring to a boil, reduce heat and put ham slices back into gravy. Simmer for 5 to 10 minutes.

Yield: 2 to 3 servings

Alice McClure
Washington

Delicious! Recipe is easily doubled for a larger group. Cooked yellow grits are great with country ham.

Country Smoked Ham

Get your country smoked ham (whatever size you want). Soak it in water over night (covered). Scrub. Put it in a large roaster with enough of this mixture to cover:

6	cups hot water (sugar dissolves better in hot water)
1	cup bourbon
1	handful sugar

You can double, triple or whatever is necessary to cover the ham with liquid. You can go ahead and simmer until you can wiggle the bone or

The way I do it is this...

Soak the ham for at least 5 to 7 days (trying to get a lot of the salt taste out. It doesn't remove all of it.) Turn the ham once a day. Change the liquid once a day. (I use inexpensive bourbon, but lots of it!)

Reduce the liquid (but reserve it), cover the pot with a lid or aluminum foil, and bake at about 325 degrees until you can wiggle the bone. When you are checking the ham, pour some of the reserved liquid over it. How long it takes depends on the size ham you purchase.

Pamela Gunnin Burkart
Washington

The bourbon helps "break down" the meat and it is so tender! I serve it always on New Year's with black-eyed peas, greens and cornbread! The leftover ham is delicious sliced paper thin and served on baby biscuits!! Now...how Southern are ya'll?!

Italian Stuffed Shells

3/4	box of jumbo shells, cooked according to directions, and drained
1	pound ground beef
1/2	pound mild Italian sausage
2	cloves garlic, minced
1	(10-ounce) box frozen chopped spinach, cooked and drained
1	(32-ounce) jar spaghetti sauce
8	ounces shredded mozzarella cheese

Brown beef, sausage and garlic. Drain well. In same skillet, put meat back in and add spinach and 1/4 cup spaghetti sauce. Mix well. Put about a cup of spaghetti sauce in bottom of 9x13-inch baking dish. Stuff shells with meat mixture and place on the spaghetti sauce in the dish. Cover with remaining sauce, sprinkle cheese on top and bake at 350 degrees, covered, for 45 minutes. Remove cover and bake about 5 minutes more. Freezes well.

Leah Pyburn
Washington

Meat Pie

1	cup cooked ham chunks
1	cup uncooked potato chunks
1	stalk celery
1	large carrot, cut to 1-inch segments
2	tablespoons chopped onions (optional)
1	can cream of potato soup
1/4	can milk
1/2	teaspoon salt
1/2	teaspoon black pepper
1/4	teaspoon oregano
1	pie crust

Cook potatoes, carrots, onions and celery until tender. Drain all but 1 inch water from pot. Add ham, potato soup and milk. Heat with vegetables. Place the mix in a deep dish pie plate. Cover with pie crust. Bake at 400 degrees for 30 to 40 minutes.

Yield: 4 to 6 servings

Mary Alice Chapin
Washington

Sausage and Wild Rice Casserole

1	(12-ounce) package bulk sausage
1	onion, chopped
8	ounces fresh mushrooms, sliced
3	cups cooked wild rice
8	eggs
1	cup milk
2	tablespoons all-purpose flour
8	ounces shredded Swiss cheese
3	tablespoons chopped parsley

You can cover and refrigerate this casserole up to 24 hours before you add the eggs. This is a fun recipe for kids because the eggs are hidden, and it surprises them. It's tasty and quite filling, nice for brunch.

Cook sausage, onions and mushrooms in frying pan until sausage is browned; drain. Add cooked wild rice and put into a greased 9x13-inch pan. With the back of a large spoon, make 8 indentations in the rice mixture. Crack one egg into each indentation. Pierce the yolks, but do not stir.

Combine milk and flour and pour over rice and eggs. Bake at 350 degrees for 30 to 40 minutes, or until eggs are set. Sprinkle with cheese. Bake an additional 2 to 3 minutes to melt cheese. Sprinkle with parsley.

Yield: 8 servings

Jan De Hoog
Terra Ceia

Sausage, Greens and Beans

1/2	pound hot or mild Italian sausage, sliced into 1/2-inch pieces
1/2	cup chopped onion
2	(19-ounce) cans of white cannellini beans, drained and rinsed
2	cups of chopped fresh spinach
3/4	cup chicken broth
1/4	cup white wine
1	teaspoon each of minced summer savory, basil, sage and rosemary
1/4	cup grated Parmesan cheese

In a large saucepan, cook the Italian sausage and onion over medium heat until the onion is tender. Drain off the fat. Add the beans, spinach, chicken broth, wine, and herbs and heat to boiling. Cover and simmer for 5 minutes. Ladle into bowls, sprinkle with Parmesan cheese and serve with crusty Italian bread and salad.

Yield: 4 servings

Vera Van Camp
Washington

Crushed fresh summer savory is said to alleviate the pain of bee stings. A few leaves of savory cooked with lima, black or lentil beans is said to eliminate the gaseous effects of these foods. Savory also goes well cooked with string beans, fried chicken and eggs.

Sweet Potato Sausage Pie

1	pound sausage meat, cooked and crumbled
1 1/2	cups apple slices, thinly cut
1 2/3	cups mashed sweet potatoes
	brown sugar
1/2	teaspoon salt
2	tablespoons butter
1/2	cup milk

Place sausage in a 9x13-inch glass baking dish. Arrange apple slices on the sausage. Sprinkle with brown sugar. Add salt, butter and milk to mashed sweet potatoes. Beat until light and fluffy. Place the sweet potato mixture over the apple slices. Bake at 350 degrees for 1 hour. Serve very hot.

Yield: 6 to 8 servings

Lexa Upton
Chocowinity

Wild Rice and Sausage Casserole

1	pound bulk pork sausage
1	cup chopped celery
1	large onion, chopped
1	green pepper, chopped
1	clove garlic, minced
3	cups chicken broth
1	can cream of mushroom soup
1	can cream of chicken soup
1	(8-ounce) can sliced water chestnuts, drained
2	(4-ounce) cans sliced mushrooms, drained
1	(6-ounce) package long grain and wild rice mix, cooked according to directions
	dash of dried thyme
1	(2-ounce) package slivered almonds

Combine first 5 ingredients in large skillet. Cook over medium heat until sausage is browned and vegetables are tender. Stir to crumble. Drain. Stir in remaining ingredients, except almonds. Mix well. Spoon into lightly greased 3-quart casserole and sprinkle with almonds. Bake at 350 degrees for 1 1/2 hours. Do not double recipe. If more is needed, make 2 separate batches.

Yield: 12 servings

Charles Bateman
Washington

(pronounced Gree-yahds)

This is a traditional New Orleans brunch dish but it can be served at any meal.

4	pounds beef or veal rounds cut 1/2-inch thick
3/4	cup oil, divided
1/2	cup all-purpose flour
1	cup chopped onions
2	cups chopped green onions
3/4	cup chopped celery
1 1/2	cups chopped green peppers
2	cloves garlic, minced
2	cups tomatoes, chopped
1/2	teaspoon tarragon, optional
2/3	teaspoon thyme
1	cup water (or less)
1	cup red wine
3	teaspoons salt
1/2	teaspoon Tabasco sauce
2	tablespoons Worcestershire sauce
3	tablespoons chopped parsley

Remove fat from meat. Cut meat into serving-size pieces. Pound to 1/4-inch thick. In a Dutch oven, brown meat well in 1/4 cup oil. As meat browns, remove to warm plate. Discard grease. To Dutch oven, add 1/2 cup oil and flour. Stir and cook to make a dark brown roux. Add onions, green onions, celery, green pepper and garlic; sauté until limp. Add tomatoes, tarragon, thyme and cook for 3 minutes. Add water and wine. Stir well, return meat. Add the salt, pepper, bay leaves, Tabasco and Worcestershire sauces. Cover and lower heat. Cook veal for one hour, beef for two hours. Remove bay leaves, stir in parsley, cool. Let sit several hours or overnight in refrigerator. More liquid may be added. Grillades should be very tender. Serve hot over grits or rice.

Johanna and Leonard Huber
Washington

Grilled Perfect Steak

Heat grill very hot.

4	1 1/2 to 2-inch thick steaks
2	sticks of unsalted butter
1/2	cup corn oil
8	teaspoons of Kosher salt
8	teaspoons of cracked black pepper

Delmonico, porterhouse – a good thick steak is required.

Melt butter. Skim milk from butter. Let cool. Remove meat from refrigerator 30 to 40 minutes before cooking. Cover with plastic wrap. Shape steak by pushing together to make thicker. Mix oil and butter in large serving plate. Coat each side of steak. Shake off excess. Press 1 teaspoon of pepper and salt into each side. Place meat on hottest part of the grill. Do not allow flare-ups — if flare-up occurs, move meat to other section of grill. Turn meat 3 times. Grill 12 minutes.

Yield: 4 to 6 servings

Dr. Pack Hindsley
Washington

Never Fail Roast Beef

This works everytime…no matter what size the roast. The trick is to not cheat and open the oven until it is done.

Preheat oven to 500 degrees. Place seasoned roast uncovered in a pan and cook:

5 minutes per pound…rare
6 minutes per pound…medium
7 minutes per pound…well done

After allotted cooking time, turn oven off and do not open for 2 hours.

Yield: 6 servings

Gray Murray
Washington

Perfect Rare Rib Roast

1   2 to 4 rib roast weighing 4 1/2 to 12 pounds
       all-purpose flour, salt and freshly ground pepper

Remove roast from refrigerator 2 1/2 to 4 hours before cooking. Preheat oven to 500 degrees.

Place roast in open, shallow roasting pan, fat side up. Sprinkle with a little flour and rub into fat lightly. Season with salt and pepper.

Put roast in oven and roast according to the roasting chart below, timing exactly. When cooking time is finished, turn off oven. Do not open door at any time. Allow roast to remain in oven until oven is lukewarm (about 2 hours). Roast will have a crunchy brown outside and an internal temperature that will be suitable for serving as long as four hours.

Roasting Chart

       2 ribs (4 1/2 to 5 pounds) .... 25 to 30 minutes
       3 ribs (8 to 9 pounds) .... 40 to 45 minutes
       4 ribs (11 to 12 pounds) ...... 55 to 60 minutes

This works out to be 15 minutes per rib or approximately 5 minutes cooking time per pound of trimmed, ready to cook roast.

To make thin pan gravy, remove excess fat from drippings. Stir in 1/2 to I cup beef broth. Bring to a boil, scraping bottom of pan. Simmer for 1 minute and season to taste.

Phyllis Encinias
Chocowinity

Filet of Beef Chasseur

8	filet mignon steaks, 6 to 8 ounces, 1 1/4 inch thick
4	large cloves garlic, peeled and crushed, divided
1 1/2	teaspoon seasoned salt
1/4	teaspoon pepper
6	tablespoons butter
2	tablespoons brandy
4	tablespoons all-purpose flour
2	teaspoons tomato paste
3/4	cup dry red wine
1	cup chicken broth
1	cup beef broth
1/2	cup water
1/2	teaspoon Worcestershire sauce
2	tablespoons currant jelly
8	ounces mushrooms, sliced

Combine half the garlic, salt and pepper to make a paste. Rub on both sides of steaks. Heat 2 tablespoons of the butter until very hot. Sauté the steaks until browned, about 1 1/2 minutes per side. The centers will be raw! Place in a 9x13-inch casserole. You may need two. Leave at least 1 inch between the steaks.

Add brandy to the skillet. Cook over medium heat, stirring constantly and scraping up brown bits from the bottom of the pan. Add remaining 4 tablespoons of butter and stir until the butter melts. Stir in the 4 tablespoons flour and stir constantly until golden. Stir in tomato paste and remaining garlic, salt and pepper. The mixture will be thick and grainy. Add the wine, broths and water. Bring to a boil, stirring constantly. Reduce heat and simmer for 10 minutes, again stirring constantly. Stir in Worcestershire and currant jelly. When jelly melts, add the sliced mushrooms.

Cool completely! Pour cooled sauce over the filets. Sauce should not come more than halfway up the sides of the steaks. Refrigerate, covered overnight. Bring to room temperature. Bake, uncovered, at 400 degrees for 20 to 30 minutes (21 minutes is perfect for medium rare).

Yield: 8 servings

Jane Page
Washington

given to me by Patricia N. Callahan,
daughter of Mary Lou Northrop,
former Washington resident

Seashell Provolone Casserole

1	large onion, finely chopped
1/4	cup margarine, melted
1 1/2	pounds lean ground beef
1	(15 1/2-ounce) jar spaghetti sauce, plain
1	(16-ounce) can stewed tomatoes
1	(4-ounce) can mushrooms, stem and pieces, drained
1	teaspoon garlic salt
1	(8-ounce) package seashell macaroni
1	(8-ounce) package provolone cheese, sliced
3	cups sour cream
1	cup shredded mozzarella cheese

Sauté onion in margarine, add beef and cook until brown, stirring to crumble meat. Add spaghetti sauce, tomatoes, mushrooms and garlic salt. Simmer 20 minutes. Cook macaroni by package directions, reducing salt, and drain. Place 1/2 of macaroni in a greased 4-quart casserole dish (or may use two 2-quart dishes). Layer with 1/2 sauce, 1/2 provolone, 1/2 sour cream. Repeat layers and top with mozzarella cheese. Cover and bake at 350 degrees for 30 minutes. Uncover and bake another 5 minutes. Let sit a few minutes before serving. May be frozen. Serve with crispy rolls and a salad.

Yield: 12 servings

Alva Douglas
Douglas Crossroads

Ann Bryan's Stuffed Bell Peppers

4	large bell peppers
4	medium Irish potatoes
1/2	stick butter
1/2	cup shredded or ground country ham
	salt and pepper taste
3/4	cup shredded cheese, optional

Remove inside of peppers and parboil peppers for 3 to 5 minutes. Cook potatoes and season. Mash with butter and add ground ham. Mix well and fill peppers with potato mixture. Place in preheated 350 degree oven and cook for 35 to 40 minutes, or until peppers are tender. Sprinkle with cheese and bake 5 minutes longer until cheese is melted.

Ann Bryan Harrington
Former Washington resident

Swiss Loaf

2	pounds ground beef
1 1/2	cups diced Swiss cheese
2	eggs, lightly beaten
1/2	cup finely chopped onions
1/2	cup finely chopped green pepper
1 1/2	teaspoons salt
1/2	teaspoon pepper
1	teaspoon celery salt
1/2	teaspoon paprika
3	cups milk
1	cup bread crumbs

Preheat oven to 350 degrees. Grease 9-inch loaf pan. (The mixture will be very soupy; I don't always get all of it into the pan.) In mixing bowl, combine all ingredients; mix well. Press into pan. Bake in preheated oven for 1 1/2 hours. (You really need to place this on a cookie tin, as it always slops over.)

Yield: 8 to 10 servings

Nannette Smyre
Chocowinity

Hamburger Casserole

1 to 1 1/2	pounds hamburger
1	medium to large onion, chopped
1	(12-ounce) can "Mexicorn", drained
1	can cream of mushroom soup
6	ounces egg noodles, cooked and drained
1	cup sour cream (8 ounces)
	salt and pepper to taste

Add onion to hamburger in large skillet, cook, stir constantly until done. Add corn, soup, noodles, sour cream, salt and pepper to hamburger mix. Put in 9x12-inch casserole dish and bake for 20 minutes.

Yield: 4 servings

Michael Deans
Aurora

Gourmet Meat Loaf

1	pound lean ground beef
1/2	pound lean ground pork
1/2	cup sour cream
1/2	cup dry bread crumbs
2	(8-ounce) cans tomato sauce
1	small jar mushrooms
1/2	cup chopped onion
2	tablespoons chopped green pepper
1	egg, beaten
2	tablespoons dry red wine
1	teaspoon salt
1/4	teaspoon pepper
2	slices bacon, cooked and crumbled
1/4	cup sour cream

Combine beef, pork, sour cream, bread crumbs, 1/2 cup tomato sauce, mushrooms, onions, green pepper, egg, wine, salt and pepper. Form into loaf. Bake at 350 degrees for 1 hour. Combine remaining sauce, bacon and sour cream. Heat, but do not boil. Serve over meat loaf.

Yield: 6 servings

Marguerite Sparrow
Washington

Peppercorn Crusted Lamb Chops

A low-fat recipe that's certain to please.

8	(4-ounce) lamb chops
2	tablespoons coarse grain mustard
1	tablespoon cracked pepper
1	green onion, finely chopped
1	tablespoon reduced sodium soy sauce
1	clove garlic
	vegetable cooking spray

Trim excess fat from chops. Combine next 5 ingredients . Spread evenly on one side of each chop. Coat grill rack with cooking spray. Place on grill over medium-hot coals (350 to 400 degrees). Place chops on rack, coated side up. Grill uncovered 5 minutes on each side until desired doneness.

Yield: 6 servings

Tucker Talley
Washington

Veal Parmesan Casserole

6   ounces spaghetti
1 1/2   pounds boneless veal round (6 serving-size pieces)
1/4   cup all-purpose flour
1/2   teaspoon salt
1/4   teaspoon pepper
1   egg, beaten
2   tablespoons milk
1/3   cup fine dry bread crumbs
1/3   cup grated Parmesan cheese
3   tablespoons cooking oil
1   large green pepper, finely chopped (1 cup)
1   large onion, finely chopped (1 cup)
2   cloves garlic, minced

You can do your own homemade tomato sauce or

2   (15-ounce) cans tomato sauce
1/4   cup water
1   teaspoon dried basil, crushed
1   cup shredded mozzarella cheese (about 6 ounces)
1/4   cup grated Parmesan cheese

You can bake the veal mixture and serve the spaghetti with sauce separately if you wish.

Break spaghetti pieces in half Cook spaghetti according to package directions; drain and set aside. Pound veal pieces to 1/4 inch thickness.

In shallow dish combine flour, salt, and pepper. In another dish combine egg and milk; in a third dish mix crumbs and the 1/3 cup Parmesan. Coat veal with flour mixture; dip in egg mixture, then in crumbs. In large skillet brown meat on both sides in hot oil, 2 or 3 pieces at a time. Remove meat, reserving drippings in skillet. In reserved drippings, cook green pepper, onion, and garlic until onion is tender. Stir in tomato sauce, water, and basil (or your homemade spaghetti sauce). Set aside 1/2 cup of the sauce; stir remaining sauce into cooked spaghetti. Turn spaghetti mixture into a 9x13-inch baking dish; arrange veal on top. Spoon reserved sauce over meat. Bake, covered, at 350 degrees for 40 minutes. Sprinkle with mozzarella and 1/4 cup Parmesan. Bake, uncovered, 10 minutes more.

Yield: 6 servings

Terri Bergevin
Washington

Veal Scallops a la Normande

8	(4-ounce) veal scallops
	salt
	white pepper
1/2	cup all-purpose flour
6	tablespoons butter, divided
1	cup cream or half and half
1/3 to 1/2	cup apple brandy

Dry eight veal scallops, each weighing 4 ounces, with paper towels. Flatten them slightly between sheets of waxed paper. Season slightly with salt and white pepper and dust with flour. In a skillet, sauté the scallops in 3 to 4 tablespoons of butter for 2 to 3 minutes on each side until lightly browned. Transfer them to a heated serving dish and keep them warm. Add 2 tablespoons butter to the skillet and return it to a moderately high heat. When the butter is melted and bubbly, stir in 2 tablespoons of flour and cook it for a minute or two but do not brown the flour. Stir in a cup of heavy cream or half and half and cook the mixture, stirring the mixture constantly until it has thickened. Add salt and white pepper to taste. Stir in approximately 1/3 to 1/2 cup of apple brandy (may use sherry or champagne). Heat and pour the sauce over the veal. It should be the thickness of a medium cream sauce.

Yield: 8 servings

Maxine C. Sandy
Washington

Osso buco
Braised Shin of Veal

4	osso buco, each weighing about 10 ounces (see above)
	all-purpose flour for dusting
3	tablespoons olive oil
1	small onion, chopped
1	small carrot, chopped
1	stalk celery, chopped
1	bay leaf
2/3	cup dry white wine
1	(14-ounce) can peeled tomatoes
1	tablespoon tomato paste
	salt
	freshly ground black pepper

Gremolata

1	clove garlic, chopped
	grated rind of 1/2 lemon
2	tablespoons chopped fresh parsley

Coat the pieces of meat with flour, handling carefully to avoid dislodging the marrow from the bones. Heat the oil in a large flameproof casserole and fry the meat quickly to seal and brown on both sides. Transfer to a plate.

Add the onion, carrot, celery and bay leaf to the pan, lower the heat and fry gently for 5 minutes, stirring occasionally. Add the wine and allow to bubble briskly until reduced by half. Add the tomatoes and their juice, the tomato paste and salt and pepper to taste. Bring to the boil, replace the meat, cover tightly and simmer gently for 1 1/2 hours until tender.

Lift out the meat, arrange in a serving dish and keep hot. Purée the vegetables with the gravy in an electric blender or pass through a sieve and, if necessary, boil briskly until reduced to a medium thick sauce. Check the seasoning and pour over the meat.

Mix the ingredients of the gremolata together and sprinkle over the meat just before serving.

Traditionally, osso buco is always accompanied by Risotto alla Milanese but no other vegetables.

Yield: 4 servings

Each portion of osso buco should be cut 2 inches thick across a leg of veal so that each piece consists of the bone complete with the marrow in the center, surrounded by meat. As suitable veal is not always readily available, it is wise to order it in advance.

If you can't find veal, you can use lamb.

Shields and I were at the Greenbrier cooking school, and Julia Child was the one who taught us this recipe.

Sandra Harvey
Washington

Veal Ragout

6	tablespoons bacon fat
4	pounds veal for stew, well trimmed of fat, cut into 1-inch cubes
2	tablespoons butter
2	large onions, chopped
3	(10-ounce) cans cream of mushroom soup
1/2	cup white wine
1	cup heavy cream
1	cup sour cream
	salt and pepper to taste
1	pound mushrooms
6	tablespoons butter
2	tablespoons chopped parsley

This stew can be made a day in advance. To serve, reheat in a 325 degree oven for 30 to 40 minutes.

Preheat oven to 300 degrees. Heat the bacon fat in skillet. Add the veal, turning pieces until they are browned on all sides. (Do not put too many pieces in the pan at once or the veal will stew without browning.) Remove the browned pieces to a large casserole.

When veal is browned, add 2 tablespoons of butter to the skillet. Cook the onions until soft, about 10 minutes. Add the soup and wine to the skillet and cook, stirring, until the soup is liquid and smooth. Add the cream and sour cream to the soup and cook until mixture is well blended. Season to taste with salt and pepper.

Pour the sauce over the veal in the casserole. Cover and bake in oven for 2 hours. Remove the stems from the mushrooms and wipe the caps clean. Just before serving, melt 6 tablespoons butter in large skillet. Sauté the mushroom caps over high heat for about 5 minutes until they are golden but not soft. To serve, arrange mushrooms caps on top of the stew and sprinkle it with parsley.

Serves 10.

Cathy Pyburn
former Washington resident

Chicken Acapulco

1	medium onion, chopped
1	tablespoon margarine
3	cups cooked chicken, cut up
2	cans cream of chicken soup
1	cup sour cream
1/2	teaspoon salt
1	large jar sliced mushrooms
1	(4-ounce) can chopped chilis
10	7-inch flour tortillas
1	cup grated sharp cheddar cheese
1/3	cup milk

Sauté onion in margarine; add chicken, one can of soup, next four ingredients. Mix. Put scoop of mixture on each tortilla, roll up; place seam side down on 9x12-inch baking dish. Combine one can soup, cheese and milk. Cover tortillas with sauce; bake at 350 degrees for 35 minutes.

Leah Pyburn
Washington

Toasted almonds may be sprinkled over dish before baking.

Pan Burritos

2	pounds ground beef
1	can enchilada sauce, divided
9	large flour tortillas
4	cups (16-ounce) shredded cheddar cheese
1	(16-ounce) can refried beans, warmed
	taco sauce, sour cream, chili peppers, chopped onions and/or guacamole

In a skillet, brown the beef. Drain, stir in one-third of the sauce. Spread another third on the bottom of a greased 9x13-inch baking pan. Place three tortillas over sauce, tearing to fit bottom of pan. Spoon half of meat mixture over tortillas; sprinkle with 1 1/2 cups cheese. Add three more tortillas. Spread refried beans over this; top with remaining meat. Sprinkle 1 1/2 cups cheese. Layer remaining tortillas; top with rest of sauce. Sprinkle the remaining cheese. Bake uncovered at 350 degrees for 35 to 40 minutes. Let stand 10 minutes before cutting. Serve with taco sauce, sour cream, peppers, onions and guacamole.

Yield: 9 servings

Dottie Lou Smith
Sidney Crossroads

Our family loves Mexican food, so this flavorful, satisfying casserole is a favorite. It's a nice way to get the taste of burritos and cut any serving size you want.

Chicken Fajitas

1/2	cup vegetable oil
1/4	cup red wine vinegar
1/3	cup lime juice
1/4	cup finely chopped onion
2	cloves garlic, minced
1	teaspoon sugar
1	teaspoon dried oregano
1/2	teaspoon salt
1/2	teaspoon pepper
1/4	teaspoon ground cumin
3	whole chicken breasts, halved, skinned and boned
8	flour tortillas
	chopped tomatoes
	shredded cheese
	shredded lettuce
	salsa
	sour cream

Combine first 10 ingredients in shallow glass bowl or large zip-top plastic bag. Mix well. Add chicken breasts and coat well. Refrigerate 4 hours. Drain chicken, reserve marinade. Grill chicken breasts, using reserved marinade to baste. Heat tortillas. Slice chicken breasts into thin slices when done. Place sliced chicken and desired garnishes on warm tortillas and roll up.

Yield: 8 servings

Margaret Dorn
Washington

Taco Pie

1	pound lean ground beef, browned and well drained
1	tablespoon chili powder
	salt
2	cloves garlic, peeled and crushed
1/4	cup sliced ripe olives
1/4	cup finely chopped onions
1	cup sour cream
2/3	cup mayonnaise
1	(8-ounce) can refrigerated crescent dinner rolls
2	tomatoes, sliced
1/4	cup sliced jalapeño peppers
1 1/2	cups shredded sharp cheddar cheese, divided

Brown meat with chili powder, salt and garlic. Drain. In a bowl, combine olives, onions, sour cream, and mayonnaise. Separate dough into 8 triangles and place in an ungreased 8 or 9 inch pie pan. Place meat and tomatoes in pie pan and sprinkle with peppers and 1 cup of cheese. Spread sour cream mix over cheese and top with rest of cheese. Bake at 375 degrees for 30 minutes. Let rest for 20 minutes prior to serving.

Yield: 8 servings

Gray Murray
Washington

I'm not sure who first made this for Nancy and me, but it was love at first bite. Every time we have ever served this, people asked for the recipe and it was passed on to them.

Quail au Vin

12	quail
	salt and pepper to taste
	all-purpose flour
8	tablespoons butter
1	cup chopped celery
1	large onion, diced
1	small bell pepper, diced
1	(10 1/2-ounce) can consommé or beef broth
1/2	cup red wine

Season quail with salt and pepper, roll in flour and brown on both sides in butter. Transfer quail to casserole; add chopped vegetables and consommé. Cook covered at 350 degrees for 2 hours. Add wine during the last 30 minutes of cooking time.

Yield: 8 servings

Alice McClure
Washington

The Pamlico, Pungo and Tar Rivers run through Beaufort County providing scenic beauty, recreational activities, fishing and crabbing. With waterfowl, deer and other wild game, bountiful gardens, wildflowers, historic homes and interesting people, Beaufort County is the place to be.

Quail or Dove

1/2	cup chopped onions
2	slices bacon, diced
1/2	cup sliced mushrooms
2	sticks (1/2 pound) butter
24	breasts of dove
3	tablespoons all-purpose flour
1	cup white wine
2	cups chicken stock
1/4	teaspoon tarragon
1/4	teaspoon basil
1/4	teaspoon chervil

Sauté onions, bacon and mushrooms in butter. Remove solid ingredients from the pan with a slotted spoon. Salt and pepper dove breasts and brown in butter. Remove breasts. Make a sauce by adding flour, wine, chicken stock, onions, bacon, mushrooms and herbs to butter. Place dove in 9x13-inch casserole dish. Pour sauce over birds. Cover and bake at 350 degrees for 30 minutes. Serve over wild rice.

Yield: 8 to 10 servings

Kathleen Taylor
Washington

Quail with Dried Beef

6	whole quail
1	(8-ounce) package dried beef in wafer-thin slices
6	strips lean bacon
1	(8-ounce) can sliced mushrooms
1	tablespoon butter or margarine
1	can of condensed cream of chicken or mushroom soup
2	tablespoons dry sherry

My husband enjoys hunting quail and we enjoy serving it. He and a friend have a game preserve and enjoy working with the dogs and being out in the wide open spaces.

Wrap each quail with strip of bacon and place in dish on piece of dried beef in one layer. Combine soup and sherry. Add small amount of milk to thin and pour over quail. Cover baking dish with aluminum foil and bake at 300 degrees for 1 1/2 hours or until tender. Uncover, increase heat to 350 degrees and bake 20 to 30 minutes, basting several times.

Note: No seasoning is suggested; black pepper may be added, but do not add salt.

Yield: 4 to 6 servings

Helen Bonner
Aurora

Texas Style Dove Breasts

24	dove halves
	jalepeño pepper slices, to taste
1	can water chestnuts, sliced
6	slices of bacon, cut lengthwise into 1/4 inch slices
	garlic, salt and black pepper to taste
	toothpicks

Season dove breasts with garlic, salt and pepper. Take a dove breast half and place 1 slice jalepeño and 1 slice water chestnut on it. Then place other breast half on top, securing with two toothpicks, one through each end, to hold the two breasts together. Wrap one thin slice of bacon around breast, holding it down with toothpicks. Place breasts on hot grill and cook until bacon is done. Do not over-cook! Carefully slide toothpicks out. The cooked bacon should hold the breasts together.

Yield: 4 to 6 servings

Doug Davis
Washington

Sherry Roasted Doves

14 to 16 doves	
	salt and pepper
1/2	cup all-purpose flour
1/2	cup salad oil
1/2	cup chopped green onions
1	cup sherry
1/4	cup chopped parsley
1 1/2	cups water

Season doves with salt and pepper. Roll in flour. Spray heavy roaster with non-stick spray, add salad oil and place doves in roaster. Bake in 400 degree oven until brown. Add onions, sherry and water. Cover, bake until tender, basting with sherry occasionally. Add parsley to gravy just before serving. Serve over rice or pasta.

Yield: 4 to 6 servings

May use quail or rabbit.

Linda Seale
Washington

Grilled Bell Bear

3 to 4 pounds of bear meat or any other wild game

Marinade

8	ounces of "Allegro" hot and spicy marinade
1/2	cup teriyaki
1/4	cup "Melinda's" hot sauce
1	tablespoon lime juice
1	onion sliced thin
2	tablespoons salt free herb-and-spice blend
1	habanero pepper, diced

Slice bear meat into strips 2x4x3/8-inches thick. Trim meat thoroughly of all fat. Combine marinade ingredients and meat and place in a one gallon freezer bag. Flatten bag and meat while removing air from bag. Refrigerate, turning bag every 6 to 8 hours. Meat can be grilled in 24 hours, but up to 3 days may be desired to add flavor and tenderness. Cook meat on medium-hot grill for 4 to 5 minutes per side or desired doneness. Be aware that marinated meats cook in less time. Can be served with a variety of sauces; mustard, hot, or seafood. Peppers and hot sauces can be altered to taste.

Yield: 12 to 16 servings, or many more sliced thinly as appetizers, hot off the grill

Wayne Tankard
Bath

Venison Back Strap

1   venison back strap (this is similar to a medium sized pork tenderloin)
2   tablespoons black pepper
      garlic and salt to taste
3   slices bacon (Cut each slice lengthwise in two. Then cut one of these slices in half lengthwise to 3/8" from the end. When pulled apart, this will make a slice that is almost double in length.)
      seasoned pepper to taste
      toothpicks

A unique entrée or appetizer!

Cover back strap with black pepper. Sprinkle with garlic salt. Wrap back strap with long strips of bacon, using three spiraled around loin one way, and the other three spiraled around the loin the other way, crisscrossing, and securing the ends with toothpicks. Sprinkle again with garlic salt and cover well with seasoned pepper pressed into the meat and bacon. Place on hot grill and cook until bacon is done. Remember that venison needs to be cooked rare to medium rare. Do not overcook! A large back strap serves 4.

Doug Davis
Washington

Texas Venison

2   pounds venison
      all-purpose flour
      salt and pepper
      vegetable oil
1   cup sliced onions
1   cup sliced celery
2   tablespoons Worcestershire sauce
2   cups stewed tomatoes
      tomato juice, optional

Cut venison into serving size pieces. Mix flour, salt and pepper to taste and coat venison with floor mixture. Heat oil in heavy iron frying pan and brown venison on both sides. Slice onions and celery and sauté until tender. Add Worcestershire sauce, stewed tomatoes and cook covered until tender. I usually add extra tomato juice. Serve over noodles or rice.

Yield: 6 to 8 servings

Helen Bonner
Aurora

Fried Beaufort County Rattler

large snake, cut in 3-inch sections
beaten egg
seafood batter mix

Good rattlesnakes are hard to come by these days, according to Wayne Tankard. Some of his snakes are brought to him by friends. He cleans the snakes, pops them in the freezer and serves them at his famous wild game dinners.

Snake needs to be at least 8 to 10 inches in circumference to provide sufficient meat. Skin snake, removing head, tail, and entrails. Cut remains into 3-inch sections. Parboil for 20 to 30 minutes depending on size. Drain and dip in beaten egg (eggbeaters work well). Roll in seafood batter and drop in oil 375 to 400 degrees. Snake will cook in 6 to 8 minutes, or until golden brown. Be aware that reptile meat is white and sweet and does not need to be overcooked. Additional seasoning can be added when done.

Wayne Tankard
Bath

Dorothy Anne Walker

Watermelon Time

watercolor

Desserts

Blueberry Almond Coffee Cake

1 1/2	cups butter
3	cups sugar
4	eggs
3	cups all-purpose flour
1	tablespoon vanilla
2	tablespoons almond extract
	pinch of salt
2	cups blueberries
	sliced almonds

Cream butter and sugar. Add eggs. Add flour, vanilla, almond extract and salt. Mix well. Gently fold in blueberries. Pour in greased 9x13-inch pan. Sprinkle with sugar and sliced almonds. Bake at 350 degrees for 45 minutes or until done.

Yield: 15 servings

Jeanne Van Staalduinen
Terra Ceia

This is a super moist coffee cake. With the fresh blueberries here in Terra Ceia, this is a family favorite every spring. In the winter, it's great to pull out those frozen blueberries and relive the memories of warmer days.

Pineapple Cupcakes

1/2	cup butter, softened
1	cup sugar
2	eggs
2	cups all-purpose flour, sifted
2	teaspoons baking powder
1/2	teaspoon salt
1	teaspoon mace
1	teaspoon nutmeg
3/4	cup milk
1	teaspoon vanilla
1/2	cup chopped pecans
1	(8-ounce) can crushed pineapple, drained

Cream butter and sugar. Add eggs and beat until smooth. Sift dry ingredients together and add alternately with milk. Add vanilla, chopped pecans and pineapple and mix until well blended. Bake at 375 degrees for 20 to 25 minutes.

Yield: 66 small cakes or 40 large cakes.

Emily Bryan Tunstall
Washington

Julia's Caramel Cake

1/2	cup butter, softened
1	cup sugar
2	eggs
3/4	cup milk
1	teaspoon vanilla
2	cups sifted all-purpose flour
2	teaspoons baking powder
1/2	teaspoon salt

Cream butter and sugar. Beat in eggs and add dry ingredients alternately with milk. Add vanilla. Pour batter in 2 eight-inch pans. Bake at 375 degrees for 25 minutes.

Betty's Birthday Caramel Icing

2	cups sugar
1	box brown sugar
1	(12-ounce) can evaporated milk
	pinch of salt
1	stick of butter, divided
1 1/2	teaspoons vanilla

Combine white and brown sugar, milk, salt and 1/3 stick of butter. Cook slowly, stirring until boiling. Let boil about one minute, or until icing reaches soft ball stage. Add 2/3 stick of butter and vanilla. Cool and beat.

Yield: 8 servings

Betty Mitchell Gray
Washington

Generally speaking, my birthday wasn't my birthday unless I got some of my mom's Caramel Cake, which is a white cake with caramel icing. For me, quite frankly, the icing was the thing. The height of my ambition was to sneak into the kitchen after we had celebrated my birthday and eat the icing off the cake, leaving a bare cake for everyone else to eat. One year, Mom gave up and made me just a sheet of caramel icing and stuck some candles in it.

Coconut Pound Cake

2	cups sugar
1	cup solid vegetable shortening
5	eggs
2	cups all-purpose flour
1 1/2	teaspoons baking powder
1	teaspoon salt
1	cup milk
1 1/2	teaspoons coconut flavoring
1	cup coconut

Cream sugar and shortening. Add eggs, one at a time, beating continuously. Mix flour, baking powder and salt and add to mixture, alternating with milk, still beating. Stir in flavoring and coconut. Pour into greased and floured Bundt pan and bake at 350 degrees for 50 minutes. Test with toothpick.

Remove from pan. While hot, using an ice pick, punch holes all over cake. Make icing and pour over cake while hot.

Icing

1	cup sugar
1/2	cup water
1	teaspoon coconut flavoring

Boil sugar and water (rolling boil) for 1 minute. Remove from heat and add the coconut flavoring. Pour slowly over cake. Cake will absorb the icing.

Yield: 8 to 10 servings

Barbara Burbage
Bath

Six Layer Orange-Coconut Cake

*North Carolina State Fair
Blue Ribbon winner for the
4 years entered!*

8	eggs, separated
1 2/3	cups sugar
3	tablespoons lemon juice
1	cup all-purpose flour
1/3	cup cornstarch
1/2	teaspoon salt
	confectioners' sugar

Have eggs at room temperature. Beat yolks until thick. Gradually beat in sugar, then 2 tablespoons lemon juice. Mix flour, cornstarch and salt and add to egg mixture. Add remaining lemon juice and beat slowly until smooth. Beat whites until stiff and fold into mixture. Spread in two 15x10-inch pans lined with waxed paper. Bake at 375 degrees for 15 to 18 minutes, or until done (cake springs back when touched with finger). If cakes do not bake evenly it may be necessary to shift pans after 10 minutes. Loosen sides of cakes from paper and turn out at once onto waxed paper sprinkled with confectioners' sugar; pull off paper. Cool. (Cake can be refrigerated several hours before frosting.) Cut each cake crosswise into 3 layers. Assemble on serving plate, spreading each layer with filling. Spread top and sides with frosting and sprinkle with orange coconut.

Orange Filling

1/2	cup all-purpose flour, sifted
1	cup sugar
1/4	teaspoon salt
1/4	cup water
1 1/4	cups orange juice
1/4	cup lemon juice
	grated orange rind
	grated lemon rind
4	egg yolks

Mix flour, sugar and salt in heavy saucepan. Add water and mix until there are no lumps. Add orange juice, lemon juice, and grated orange and lemon rind. Cook over low heat until mixture thickens and becomes almost translucent. Beat egg yolks slightly; add hot mixture slowly, stirring constantly. Return to saucepan and cook slowly, stirring constantly, a few minutes longer. Cool.

(continued)

Fluffy Frosting

1	cup sugar
1/4	teaspoon cream of tartar
1/8	teaspoon salt
1/3	cup hot water
3	egg whites

Combine first 4 ingredients in saucepan. Cook, without stirring, to 240 degrees on candy thermometer. Meanwhile beat egg whites until stiff but not dry. Add syrup slowly to egg whites, beating constantly until frosting holds its shape.

Orange Coconut

1	large orange
1	(3 1/2-ounce) can of flaked coconut

Grate rind of 1 large orange, being careful not to get any of the white part of orange. With fingertips, mix with coconut until tinted orange.

Yield: 10 to 12 servings.

Ann Peters
Washington

Cream Cheese Poundcake

1	stick butter, softened
8	ounces cream cheese
1	cup sugar
4	eggs
1/2	cup oil
1	cup all-purpose flour
1	package butter cake mix
2/3	cup evaporated or whole milk

Cream together butter and cream cheese. Add sugar, eggs and oil. Fold in flour and cake mix. Then add milk and mix well.

Spray a tube pan with vegetable cooking spray and pour in batter. Bake at 300 degrees for 1 hour (may require extra 10 to 20 minutes).

Yield: 10 servings

Charlene Alligood, Nancy Murray, Virgil Stewart, Margaret Woolard
Washington

"Try Cake"

In the 1930s, my grandmother would mix cake batters (with no measuring) and then bake a small portion of the batter in a tart tin to "try it out." Then she could correct the texture and I would get the sample. This was called the "Try Cake."

Nancy Collis

Amaretto Cake

2	packages Stella D'oro almond toast
1	(3-ounce) package chocolate pudding (not instant)
1	(3-ounce) package vanilla pudding (not instant)
3 1/2	cups milk, divided
1/2	cup amaretto liqueur, divided
	large package frozen non-dairy whipped topping
2	packages slivered almonds

Amaretto is an almond-flavored liqueur first produced in Sarrono, Italy. Often, it is made with the kernels of apricot pits.

Butter springform pan. Cover bottom of pan with one layer of almond toast, placed on side and not upright.

Mix vanilla pudding with 1 3/4 cups milk and 1/4 cup amaretto. Microwave for 2 minutes, stir, and return to microwave. Cook for 2 minutes, stir and return to microwave. Cook for another 2 minutes. (Total cooking time - 6 minutes.) Pour over toast in pan.

Place another layer of toast over vanilla pudding.

Cook chocolate pudding, following same procedure. Pour over second layer of toast. Pan will be full. Cover with plastic wrap and foil and refrigerate. Must be made at least one day before serving.

Sauté almonds with small amount of butter in a frying pan, stirring constantly until dark brown. DO NOT BURN.

Cool almonds. Release cake from springform pan onto cake plate and ice with whipped topping. Place almonds over top and sides of cake. Must keep cake refrigerated.

Yield: 8 or more servings

Helen Sommerkamp
Aurora

Almond Cake

1/2	pound butter or margarine, softened
1	cup sugar
1	egg
1	teaspoon vanilla
2	cups all-purpose flour
1/2	teaspoon baking soda
1/2	teaspoon salt

Filling

1	cup almond paste (can be bought at the Terra Ceia Christian School)
2	eggs
1	cup sugar

Cream together first four ingredients. Sift together dry ingredients and add to creamed mixture to make batter. Place 1/2 batter in 9x13-inch greased pan. Pat down and up side of pan a little.

Mix filling ingredients. Spread all filling over batter. This is hard to spread, so take a little in your hand, flatten it out and put over batter. Do this until filling is used and batter is covered. Pour remaining half of batter over filling, spreading to cover as much as possible. While baking, batter will spread out.

Bake at 350 degrees for 40 to 45 minutes. When cool, cut into squares. Freezes well.

Yield: 15 servings

Agnes Kuiken
Pinetown

Chocolate Cake

3	cups sifted all-purpose flour
2 1/2	cups sugar
1/2	teaspoon salt
1 1/2	cups buttermilk
3/4	cup solid vegetable shortening
1 1/2	teaspoons vanilla
3	squares unsweetened baking chocolate, melted
3	eggs
1 1/2	teaspoons soda, mixed with 1 1/2 teaspoons vinegar

In large mixing bowl, beat first 6 ingredients for 2 minutes. Add melted chocolate, and beat for 2 more minutes. Add eggs, beat 2 minutes. Add soda and vinegar mixture and beat 2 minutes.

Grease and flour 2 9-inch round cake pans. Cut a circle of wax paper to cover bottom of pans. Fill with batter and bake at 350 degrees for about 50 minutes.

Icing

4	cups sifted confectioners' sugar
1/2	cup cream
6	tablespoons melted butter
2	squares melted chocolate
1	teaspoon vanilla

Mix all ingredients and beat until consistency to spread.

Yield: 8 to 10 servings

Margaret Dorn
Washington

During the early 30s and 40s, some of the best cakes in Washington were made at the home of Mrs. Fred Ayers. Affectionately known as "Miss Annie Mae", her cakes were rich with real butter and fresh eggs and always delicious. As a member of the Jim Hackney family, she often made their favorites, a devil's food and a lemon-orange cake. For small children, she made a "Rabbit" birthday cake, decorated with her homemade marshmallow rabbits placed around the sides. All children wanted a rabbit cake.

Elegant Lemon Cake Roll

4   eggs, separated and at room temperature
3/4   cup sugar, divided
1   tablespoon vegetable oil
1   teaspoon lemon extract
1/2   cup sugar
2/3   cup sifted cake flour
1   teaspoon baking powder
1/4   teaspoon salt
1 to 2 tablespoons confectioners' sugar

Bath is the home of the oldest Episcopal church in the state. Many of its charming historic homes are opened for tours during the Christmas season, at which time colonial cooking is demonstrated.

Grease bottom and sides of a 10x15-inch jelly roll pan; line with wax paper, grease and flour the paper. Set aside.

Beat egg yolks in a large bowl at high speed with an electric mixer until thick and lemon colored; gradually add 1/4 cup sugar, beating constantly. Stir in vegetable oil and lemon extract; set aside.

Beat egg whites until foamy; gradually add 1/2 cup sugar, beating until stiff but not dry. Fold whites into yolks. Combine flour, baking powder and salt; gradually fold into egg mixture. Spread batter evenly in prepared pan. Bake at 350 degrees for 10 to 12 minutes.

Sift confectioners' sugar in a 10x15-inch rectangle on a towel. When cake is done, immediately loosen from sides of pan and turn out on sugared towel. Carefully peel off wax paper. Start at narrow end and roll up cake and towel together. Let cool completely on a wire rack, seam side down.

Creamy Lemon Filling

1   (14-ounce) can sweetened condensed milk
1 to 2 teaspoons grated lemon rind
3   lemons, juiced
2   cups non-dairy whipped topping
1   cup coconut

Combine first three ingredients. Blend in whipped topping.

Unroll cake. Spread with half of filling. Carefully reroll cake without towel. Place cake on plate, seam down; spread remaining filling on all sides. Sprinkle with coconut.

Yield: 10 to 12 servings

Nan Hawkins
Bath

Italian Cream Cheese Cake

1	stick margarine, softened
1/2	cup shortening
2	cups sugar
5	egg yolks
2	cups all-purpose flour
1	teaspoon soda
1	cup buttemilk
1	teaspoon vanilla
1	cup coconut
1	cup pecans, chopped
5	egg whites, stiffly beaten

Combine margarine and shortening. Add sugar and beat well. Add egg yolks and continue beating. Mix flour and soda together, and add alternately with buttermilk to egg mixture. Stir in vanilla and add coconut and pecans. Fold in stiffly beaten egg whites.

Pour into three greased and floured 9-inch layer pans and bake at 350 degrees for 20 to 25 minutes, or until cake layers test done.

Cream Cheese Frosting

1	(8-ounce) package cream cheese
1/2	stick margarine
1	box confectioners' sugar
1	teaspoon vanilla flavoring
	milk
	chopped nuts, if desired

Beat cream cheese and margarine until smooth. Add sugar and mix well. Add vanilla. Thin with a few drops of milk, if necessary. Spread over layers, top and sides of cake. Sprinkle top with nuts.

Yield: 10 to 12 servings

Richard Potter
Chocowinity

Pumpkin Cheesecake

Yummy at Thanksgiving!

Crust

1 1/2   cups graham crackers crumbs
1/4   cup sugar
1/3   cup butter or margarine, melted

Combine ingredients and put mixture in oiled 9-inch springform pan.

Bake at 350 degrees for 6 to 8 minutes. Do not brown.

Filling

3   (8-ounce) packages cream cheese
1   cup sugar
1/4   cup brown sugar, firmly packed
1 3/4   cups (15-ounce can) solid pack pumpkin
2   eggs
2/3   cup evaporated milk
2   tablespoons cornstarch
1 1/4   teaspoons ground cinnamon
1/2   teaspoon nutmeg

Beat cream cheese with sugars until fluffy. Add pumpkin, eggs, evaporated milk, cornstarch, cinnamon and nutmeg. Mix well. Bake at 350 degrees for 55 to 60 minutes.

Topping

2   cups (16-ounce container) sour cream, room temperature
1/4 to1/3 cup sugar
1   teaspoon vanilla
        ground cinnamon
        cinnamon sticks

Combine ingredients and mix until smooth. Spread topping over warm cheesecake and bake at 350 degrees for 8 minutes. Cool on wire rack. Chill for several hours or overnight. Remove pan and garnish with ground cinnamon and cinnamon sticks.

Yield: 10 servings

Emily Mayne
Washington

Apricot Nectar Cake

Cake

1	box yellow cake mix
1/2	cup sugar
4	eggs
1	cup apricot nectar
3/4	cup cooking oil

Mix cake mix, sugar, eggs, apricot nectar and cooking oil until well blended, Pour in tube pan and bake at 360 degrees for 30 or 40 minutes.

Topping

2	tablespoons lemon juice
1/2	cup apricot nectar
1	cup confectioners' sugar

Combine lemon juice, apricot nectar and confectioners' sugar and stir until thoroughly blended. Pour topping over hot cake.

Yield: 10 to 12 servings

Roy Tucker
Chocowinity

Never Fail Caramel Icing

This was given to me by Ella Rees Wilkinson.

1	stick butter
1	cup brown sugar
1/4	cup whole milk
	confectioners' sugar

Melt butter in saucepan. Add brown sugar and milk. Cook over medium heat for 3 minutes. Stir constantly until mixture boils up big fluffy bubbles. Remove from heat and let cool completely. Add confectioners' sugar until consistency is slightly loose, not drippy or stiff. Use immediately to ice cakes.

Note: Double this if you want to ice large cake or like lots of icing.

Mavis Rodman Peele
Washington

Manilla's Chocolate Frosting

1   box confectioners' sugar
5   tablespoons cocoa
         dash of salt
1   stick butter, softened
1   lemon, juiced
1   tablespoon vanilla
1/4   teaspoon maple flavoring
1 to 2 teaspoons milk

Mix sugar, cocoa, salt together. Add butter, lemon juice and mix. Add flavorings and continue to mix. Add small amount of milk, if necessary, for spreading.

Rita P. Tetterton
Washington

Mama's chocolate frosting is simple to make, but very good.

Boiled Chocolate Icing

2   cups sugar
1/2   cup evaporated milk or one (5-ounce) can
6   tablespoons cocoa, heaping
1   stick butter
1   teaspoon vanilla
         pinch of salt

Mix all ingredients, except vanilla. Bring to a boil over medium heat. When it begins to boil, stir occasionally for 2 minutes. Remove from heat, add vanilla. Cool and beat. Pour over cake.

Joe Phillips
Aurora

If you cook this a little longer, this will make an excellent fudge. You may add nuts.

Raspberry Topping

1   (10-ounce) package frozen raspberries
1/4   cup sugar
1   tablespoon cornstarch
1/3   cup water
         dash of salt
1   tablespoon lemon juice (fresh, strained)

Combine first five ingredients and mix in heavy saucepan. Cook over medium heat. Boil about 2 minutes, stirring constantly. Remove from heat. Stir in fresh lemon juice. Chill.

Sue Graves
Washington

Serve over vanilla ice cream. For a special flair, serve in baked meringues.

Blueberry Pie with Crème Chantilly

4	cups fresh blueberries, washed, divided
3/4	cup sugar
1/2	cup water
2	tablespoons cornstarch, dissolved in 2 tablespoons water
1	tablespoon butter
4	tablespoons Cointreau liqueur
1/4	cup slivered almonds, toasted
1	9-inch deep dish pie shell, baked

Combine 1 cup blueberries, sugar, and water in blender and purée until smooth. Pour mixture into medium saucepan and add dissolved cornstarch. Heat until thickened, stirring frequently. Stir in butter and Cointreau. Add almonds and remaining blueberries, stirring gently to combine. Pour into baked pie shell and chill.

Crème Chantilly

1	cup heavy cream, whipped
2	tablespoons sugar
1/4	teaspoon almond extract

Combine cream, sugar, and almond extract in chilled small bowl and whip until stiff peaks form. Just before serving, spread on top of chilled pie.

Yield: 8 servings

Jean Shook
Chocowinity

In the first half of the 1900s, huckleberry bushes grew wild. It took hundreds to make just one pie because they were so small but delicious. Similar to the blueberry, but much tastier, they looked like blue-black jewels, and were brought into town and sold door to door by the bucketful. Few plants, if any, survive today.

German Chocolate Pie

1	8-inch graham cracker crumb crust, baked
1	(4-ounce) sweet German chocolate bar
1/3	cup milk, divided
2	tablespoons sugar
1	(3-ounce) package cream cheese, softened
1	(8-ounce) non-dairy whipped topping

Heat chocolate and 2 tablespoons milk over low heat. Beat sugar into cream cheese. Add remaining milk and chocolate mixture and beat until smooth. Fold mixture into whipped topping, blending until smooth. Spoon into crust. Freeze until firm, about 4 hours.

Yield: 8 servings

Nancy De Hoog
Terra Ceia

The Terra Ceia Dutch Festival (at one time, the "Tulip Festival" in Washington) was held yearly in the spring to celebrate the blooming of the Dutch bulbs and consuming Dutch foods.

Fluffy Cranberry Cream Pie

1	9-inch baked pastry shell
2	(3-ounce) packages cream cheese, softened
1	(14-ounce) can sweetened condensed milk
1/2	cup frozen cranberry juice cocktail concentrate, thawed
2	tablespoons bottled lemon juice
	red food coloring, optional
1	cup (1/2 pint) whipping cream, whipped
	Cranberry Topping

In large mixer bowl, beat cream cheese until fluffy. Gradually beat in sweetened condensed milk until smooth. Add juice concentrate, lemon juice and food coloring if desired. Fold in whipped cream. Pour into prepared pastry shell. Chill 3 hours or until set. Garnish with Cranberry Topping. Serve with additional topping.

Great for the holidays.

Cranberry Topping

1	(16-ounce) can whole cranberry sauce
1/4	cup frozen cranberry juice cocktail concentrate, thawed
1	tablespoon cornstarch

In medium saucepan, combine ingredients. Over medium heat, cook and stir until thickened and clear. Cool. Chill thoroughly. (Makes about 2 cups).

Yield: 8 servings

Irene Forbes
Washington

Apple Jonathan

4   cups peeled apple slices
1/2   cup cider
1/2   teaspoon cinnamon
1/8   teaspoon cloves
1/8   teaspoon nutmeg
1   cup light brown sugar, firmly packed
1/4   cup butter

Arrange sliced apples in buttered baking dish or pie plate. Add cider. Mix spices with sugar and sprinkle over apples. Dot with butter. Cover apples with biscuit dough. Make slits in dough with knife for steam to escape. Bake at 350 degrees for 30 minutes or until apples are tender. Cooking time depends upon texture and quality of apples. Serve warm with vanilla ice cream if desired.

Biscuit dough

2   cups all-purpose flour
5   teaspoons baking powder
1/2   teaspoon salt
1/4   cup butter, softened
3/4   cup milk

Sift first three dough ingredients and cut in butter until mixture resembles a pea. Add milk and mix until blended. Toss on a flour board. Roll to a 1/4 inch thickness.

Yield: 8 servings

Doris Miller Galuszka
Washington

Cranberry Apple Pie

Pastry

4	cups all-purpose flour
1	tablespoon sugar
2	teaspoons salt
1 3/4	cups solid vegetable shortening
2 to 3	tablespoons ice water
1	large egg
1	tablespoon cider vinegar

Combine flour, sugar and salt in large bowl. With pastry blender or two knives cut in shortening until mixture resembles coarse crumbs. Whisk water, egg and vinegar in cup. Sprinkle onto flour mixture, 1 tablespoon at a time, tossing with a fork and adding more water as needed until pastry holds together. Divide into 4 balls; flatten into disks. Wrap and refrigerate 1 hour. (Reserve 2 pastry disks for another use. Wrap and freeze up to 1 month.)

Filling

3/4	cup firmly packed brown sugar
1/4	cup sugar
1/3	cup all-purpose flour
1	teaspoon cinnamon
4	cups peeled, sliced Granny Smith or other tart baking apples
2	cups chopped cranberries
2	tablespoons butter, cut up
1/2	cup heavy or whipping cream

Combine sugars, flour and cinnamon in large bowl. Add fruit and stir until well-coated. Preheat oven to 425 degrees. On lightly floured surface, roll one pastry disk (with a floured rolling pin) into a 12-inch circle. Fit into a 9-inch pie plate, leaving 1 inch overhang. Spoon in filling and dot with butter. Brush overhang with water. Roll second pastry disk into 11-inch circle. Cut vents. Place over filling. Trim and flute edge.

Bake pie 15 minutes. Reduce oven temperature to 350 degrees. Bake 50 minutes, or until apples are tender and filling is bubbly. (If pastry browns too quickly, cover loosely with foil.) With knife, re-cut vents. Pour cream through vents. Bake 5 minutes.

Note: You may substitute 2 cups of apples for the 2 cups of cranberries. Adding the cream at the end of the recipe is also an option. It's delicious either way.

Yield: 8 servings

Jean Gerard Lee
Washington

This pie won first prize when members of the House of Representatives were asked to submit a favorite family recipe for apple pie. This garnet-colored pie is the creation of Republican Congressman Scott Klug's wife, Tess. She used her mother's crust recipe and combined two of her favorite pie recipes. The McLaughlin Group, whose diverse viewpoints make for TVs liveliest political debates, were ask to judge the pies. At this particular time the Democrats were in the majority. Their consensus: The Democrats may hold the majority in Congress, but the Republicans bake the best pies.

Best of the Best Lemon Meringue Pie

This is one pie that's worth the effort. None of this easy lemon pie filling stuff. You'll be glad you tried it.

2	graham cracker pie shells, baked
2 1/4	cups sugar
2 1/4	cups water
3/4	teaspoon salt
3/4	cup cornstarch
1/2	cup water
6	egg yolks, slightly beaten
3/4	cup lemon juice
4 1/2	tablespoons butter

Combine sugar, water and salt in saucepan. Heat until boiling. Mix cornstarch and water. Pour cornstarch mixture slowly into boiling water, stirring constantly. Cook until thick and clear, stirring constantly as it thickens, so that it doesn't stick to bottom of pan. Combine egg yolks and lemon juice. Stir into thickened mixture. Continue to heat and cook, stirring constantly, until mixture bubbles. Remove from heat and stir in butter. Cover and cool until lukewarm.

Meringue

1/4	teaspoon salt
6	egg whites
3/4	cup sugar

Add salt to egg whites and beat until frothy. Add sugar and beat until stiff peaks form. Mix 2 rounded tablespoons of meringue into the lemon filling. Pour filling into the shells. Spread remaining meringue on top. Bake at 325 degrees for 15 minutes, or until meringue is light brown. Cool I hour before serving.

Yield: 8 servings

Jan De Hoog
Terra Ceia

Sweet Potato Pie

1 1/2   cups mashed sweet potatoes
2/3   cup sugar
2   tablespoons melted butter
1/2   teaspoon nutmeg
1/2   teaspoon mace
1/2   teaspoon vanilla
1 1/2   teaspoon salt
2   teaspoons lemon juice
3   eggs, beaten
        grated rind of one lemon
1 1/4   cup of brandy or Frangelica liquor
3/4   cup heavy cream
1   pie crust, baked

Bake pie crust for 10 minutes at 375 degrees. Then increase oven temperature to 450 degrees while mixing pie filling. Mix sweet potatoes and sugar. Add the rest of the ingredients. Pour into baked pie crust and put in hot oven. Lower temperature to 375 degrees and bake for 35 to 40 minutes or until knife inserted in the center comes out clean.

Serve with a dollop of whipped cream on top of each slice.

Yield: 8 servings

Pamela Gunnin Burkart
Washington

This recipe was given to me by Claudia Hackney (Mrs. Kenneth) of Washington many years ago. I love it served warm with the whipped cream! Sinfully delicious...maybe it's the Frangelica!?

Macaroon Pie

14 to 16   saltine crackers, crushed
12   dates, chopped
1   cup pecans, chopped
3   egg whites, beaten stiffly
1   cup sugar
1   teaspoon almond extract

Mix first three ingredients. Beat egg whites until stiffened and add sugar and almond flavoring. Fold into nut/cracker mix. Pour into greased pie plate. Bake at 350 degrees for 20 to 25 minutes.

Yield: 8 servings

Ann Windley
Aurora

Egg Nog Pie

1 1/3 cups crushed graham crackers (7 double)
1/4 cup sugar
1/4 teaspoon nutmeg
1/4 teaspoon cinnamon
1/4 cup butter, melted
2 eggs
1/8 teaspoon salt
1 1/3 cups sugar, divided
1 package unflavored gelatin
1/3 cup dark rum
2 cups heavy whipping cream
dash of nutmeg

Mix graham crackers, sugar, nutmeg, cinnamon and butter and pat into either a 9-inch or 10-inch pie plate. Bake at 375 degrees for 8 minutes. Cool to room temperature.

Combine eggs, salt and 2/3 cup sugar in small bowl and beat until well mixed. Set bowl in pan of hot water and continue beating for 5 minutes. Soften gelatin in rum. Let sit for 5 minutes.

Beat gelatin into egg mixture and remove bowl from hot water.

In large bowl, beat whipping cream, 2/3 cup sugar and nutmeg. When stiff, gently fold egg mixture into cream. Pour into pie shell. Sprinkle with nutmeg and freeze.

This doesn't get real hard so remove just when ready to serve. Will make one large 9-inch pie or one nice-sized 10-inch pie.

Yield: 8 servings

Leah Pyburn
Washington

Danish Puff

1/2   **cup butter, softened**
1   **cup all-purpose flour**
2   **tablespoons water**

Cut butter into flour. Sprinkle water over the flour/butter mixture and mix with hands. Form dough into a ball; divide in half. Pat the divided dough into two flat strips on an ungreased baking sheet.

1/2   **cup butter**
1   **cup water**
1   **teaspoon almond extract**
1   **cup all-purpose flour**
3   **eggs**

Heat butter and water to a rolling boil. Remove from heat and stir in almond extract and flour. Stir vigorously over low heat until mixture forms a ball. Remove from heat; add eggs and beat until smooth. Spread batter evenly over the two strips of pastry. Bake at 350 degrees until topping is crisp and browned, about 55 minutes. Cool. Spread with confectioners' sugar glaze and toasted sliced almonds.

Glaze

1 1/2   **cups confectioners' sugar**
2   **tablespoons butter**
1 to 2   **tablespoons warm milk**
1 1/2   **teaspoons almond extract**
        toasted almonds
        maraschino cherries (optional)

Beat sugar and butter until smooth. Add warm milk until spreading consistency. Add almond extract and spread glaze evenly on top of the baked pastry. Sprinkle with toasted almonds. Small pieces of maraschino cherries may be added.

Yield: 10 to 12 servings

Pat Hill
Washington

Hobart and Flora Belle Brown began the Brownie Bakery in 1947 and remained in business for more than 45 years. Flora Belle recalls that their first customer was Frances Roberson who ordered a devil's food cake; and the second order was a pecan pie for Guy Swindell. The Browns originated the "Brownie Biscuit", which was actually a yeast roll dough cut with a biscuit cutter, hence the name. Elaborately decorated birthday and wedding cakes, cinnamon rolls and coconut macaroons were specialties.

English Toffee Dessert

3/4	cup sugar
1/2	cup whipping cream
1/4	cup light corn syrup
2	tablespoons butter
1/2	cup crushed chocolate covered toffee candy
2	pints fresh strawberries
	sour cream

Combine first 4 ingredients in small saucepan. Boil for one minute. Remove from heat, stir in candy and cool. Serve sauce over strawberries topped with sour cream.

Note: Sauce will keep for several weeks in refrigerator.

Yield: 6 to 8 servings

Sue Nicholson
Bath

In the 1930s, ladies' bridge parties were held after dinner, and the ladies were expected to wear their finest long gowns. Elegant desserts and coffee were served.

Angelic Orange Dessert

	slices of angel food cake (a flat slice works best)
1	quart vanilla ice cream
	Orange Sauce
4	ounces almonds, toasted and chopped
8	ounces whipped cream or non-dairy whipped topping

Place 1 slice of angel food cake on each plate. Top with 2 scoops of vanilla ice cream. Cover with orange sauce, top with toasted almonds and a dollop of whipped cream.

Orange Sauce

4	tablespoons butter
1	cup sugar
1	egg
1/2	cup freshly squeezed orange juice

Cream butter and sugar together and whisk in egg and orange juice. Cook over very low heat until thick, about 5 minutes. Sauce can be served hot or cold.

Yield: 10 to 12 servings

Hester Anne Kidd
Washington

This is to die for! I served this dessert for a bridge party (6 tables) that I had in Warrenton, N.C. when Bill first started his dental practice there in 1953. A way to pay back all those nice ladies who had invited me into their homes.

Lemon Custard Cake Cups

1	lemon
2	tablespoons butter
1	cup sugar
4	tablespoons all-purpose flour
	pinch salt
3	eggs, separated
1 1/2	cups milk
8	ounces whipped cream

Grate rind and juice lemon. Cream butter and sugar. To this add flour, salt, juice and rind. Add beaten egg yolks that have been mixed with the milk. Fold in stiffly beaten egg whites. Pour into 8 greased custard cups. Place cups in a pan of 1-inch deep hot water. Bake at 350 to 375 degrees for 45 minutes. To turn out, run small spatula around edges. May serve in custard cups. Serve with dollops of whipped cream. As this cooks, the custard forms on the top while a cake forms on the bottom. May serve warm or cold.

Yield: 8 servings

Gale Champion
Washington

Cranberry Swirl

2	cups heavy whipping cream
2	tablespoons sugar
1	tablespoon Grand Marnier (do not use Triple Sec), optional
1/4	cup fresh orange zest
1	can whole berry cranberry sauce

In a large bowl, whip cream until it starts to thicken. Add sugar and continue beating until it thickens more; add Grand Marnier and beat until creamy, fluffy and holds peaks. In another bowl, blend the orange zest into the cranberry sauce. Then gently fold into the cream with a rubber spatula. Cream should be pink and white marbled. Pour into glass punch cups or stemmed glasses to serve.

Yield: 8 servings

Louise Lane
Washington

This is easy, pretty and good. Nice with a minted garnish.

Mercer Island Thrower-Downer

Takes care of dessert, coffee and after-dinner drink

3   ounces bourbon
2   cups black coffee at room temperature
4   scoops of vanilla ice cream

Place all in blender, mix on medium speed and serve in parfait glasses.

Yield: 6 servings

Leonard V. Huber
Washington

Pavlova

I brought this recipe from New Zealand and have enjoyed it very much.

4 to 5   egg whites, room temperature
1 1/4   cup sugar
1   teaspoon vanilla
2   teaspoons vinegar
2   teaspoons cornstarch
     whipped cream or whipped topping
     bowl of fruit, cut into bite-sized pieces

Grease round section on cookie sheet (the size of a cake pan) and sprinkle with sugar. Beat egg whites until stiff and add sugar, vanilla, vinegar and cornstarch. Pile mixture on round section and flatten as much as possible. Bake at 200 degrees for 2 hours. Turn off oven and leave cake inside to cool. Place fruit and cream on top of cake, or serve on cut wedges.

Note: The fruit may be anything in season that you like. Add a little sugar to the fruit, if desired.

Yield: 8 servings

Helen Sommerkamp
Aurora

Lemon Angel Torte

4	egg whites, reserving yolks for sauce
1	cup sugar, divided
1/4	teaspoon salt
1/4	teaspoon cream of tartar
1	cup heavy cream, whipped stiffly
1	recipe Lemon Filling

Preheat oven to very hot (450 degrees). Place egg whites, 3/4 cup sugar, salt and cream of tartar in small mixing bowl. Beat whites at high speed until very stiff peaks form. Spread in well-greased 9-inch pie plate. Place in preheated oven. Now turn off heat and let stand in closed oven 5 hours or over night (do not peek). Whip cream, sweeten with 1/4 cup sugar. Fill torte with half of the whipped cream, then with Lemon Filling. Top with remaining cream. Chill 5 hours.

Lemon Filling

4	egg yolks
1/2	cup sugar
	dash of salt
1	tablespoon grated lemon peel
3	tablespoons lemon juice

In top of double boiler, beat egg yolks until thick and lemon-colored. Gradually beat in sugar, dash of salt, lemon peel, and lemon juice. Cook over simmering water, stirring constantly, until thick (about 3 to 4 minutes). Cool.

Yield: 8 servings

Leah Pyburn
Washington

This recipe always receives raves from my Book Club!

Pot de Crème

1	cup chocolate bits
1	egg
2	tablespoons sugar
2	tablespoons rum
3/4	cup hot scalded milk (this cooks the egg)
1	cup heavy cream, whipped

My cousin Ruth, a chocolate addict, said "It's too easy; can't be good!" But she changed her mind when she tried this!

Put all ingredients into blender and mix well. Pour into serving dishes. Chill. You can make this a day ahead. Serve with whipped cream. Use the "real" stuff, if you dare! Add a little shaving of chocolate.

Note: Make only one recipe at a time.

Yield: 4 servings

Judy Kidwell
Washington

Caramel Pecan Ice Cream

1 1/4	cups sugar, divided
6	egg yolks
2	cups half and half
2	cups whipping cream
2	teaspoons vanilla
2	tablespoons water
1 1/2	cups pecans, toasted and chopped

Miss Mollie Vines had the first ice cream parlor in Washington. In the front of her store, she sold hats. In the rear was her ice cream parlor.

Put egg yolks and 3/4 cup sugar in bowl and beat until mixture is pale yellow. Bring the half and half and whipping cream to a boil in a saucepan. Add 1/2 cup of hot cream to the sugar/yolk mixture and stir. Pour into remaining cream mixture in saucepan and cook until almost a boil (180 degrees). In a separate saucepan, heat water and remaining 1/2 cup of sugar over medium heat, stirring until it turns an amber brown. Do not burn. Place about a cup of custard into the caramelized sugar. Mix well and pour sugar into custard mixture, stirring all ingredients together. Put this mixture into cold bowl and cool to room temperature. Add vanilla. Pour custard into the canister of your favorite ice cream maker and proceed to freeze as directed. Stir in pecans when ice cream is partially frozen. Put ice cream mixture in a freezer container and store in freezer .

Sue Nicholson
Bath

Steamed Ginger Pudding with White Sauce

1	cup all-purpose flour
6	tablespoons butter, melted
1/4	cup sugar
1	teaspoon ground ginger
1/2	cup dark corn syrup
1	egg, beaten
1/4	teaspoon soda
3	tablespoons milk

Heat oven to 350 degrees. Butter or spray pudding mold or a bowl.

Sift flour, then add butter, sugar and ginger. Stir in syrup, egg and last, the soda mixed with milk. Pour batter into mold or bowl and cover. Note: depending on mold or bowl size, recipe may be doubled. Basic recipe makes four small servings.

Place pudding on a steamer rack in a large pan with at least 1-inch of simmering water. Cover. Steam for 1 1/4 to 1 3/4 hours. Check water level frequently. I prefer moist pudding and test cooking time by inserting small wooden skewer. Remove from pan and keep warm for serving, or cool, then refrigerate and reheat for serving later. Serve with warm white sauce

White Sauce

2	tablespoons butter
2	tablespoons all-purpose flour
2	tablespoons sugar
1/2 to 1	teaspoon vanilla
1/2 to 1	cup milk

Melt butter in medium pan. Add flour and remaining ingredients. Stir constantly over low to medium heat until thick. Top servings of pudding with warm sauce and enjoy!

Yield: 4 servings

Wanda Johnson
Washington

This recipe is from my Yorkshire, England, grandmother Bessie England Townend. My mother, Betty Townend Holladay, served it each Christmas. A wonderful aroma filled the house as the pudding steamed.

My Favorite Brownies

1	cup butter
2	cups sugar
4	eggs
1/2	cup cocoa
1	cup all-purpose flour
1/8	teaspoon salt
1	tablespoon vanilla
1	cup chopped pecans
3/4	package miniature marshmallows
	Icing

Cream together butter, sugar and eggs. Add remaining ingredients. Blend and pour into 9x13-inch pan. Sprinkle with chopped pecans. Bake at 350 degrees for 30 to 35 minutes. After 35 minutes, turn off oven. Remove pan and put 3/4 package miniature marshmallows on top. Return to oven and leave while you make icing. The marshmallows should puff.

Icing

1	cup butter
1	box confectioners' sugar
3	tablespoons cocoa, heaping
1/3	cup milk

Combine. Heat until mixed and pour over pan full of brownies. Cool.

Yield: 18 servings

Beth Page
Washington

Lemon Madeleines

1/2 cup butter
3/4 cup sugar
2 large eggs
1/4 cup plain low-fat yogurt
1 teaspoon lemon extract
1/2 teaspoon vanilla
1 cup all-purpose flour
1 teaspoon grated lemon peel
1/4 teaspoon salt
confectioners' sugar

Melt butter over low heat and set aside. In a large bowl with mixer, beat eggs, sugar, yogurt and lemon and vanilla extracts until blended, occasionally scraping bowl. Increase speed, beating until very light and lemon colored (about 5 minutes). Reduce to low speed and beat in flour, grated lemon peel, salt and melted butter until well blended. Spoon into greased madeleine shells. Bake at 400 degrees for 10 to 15 minutes. Remove from pan immediately and sprinkle with confectioners' sugar. Store in tightly covered container.

Jan Israel
Chocowinity

Marcel Proust brought lasting fame to this shell-shaped cookie when he described eating one in his classic novel, "Remembrance of Things Past."

Cherry Fruit Chews

1/4 cup margarine or butter, softened
1 cup sugar
2 eggs
1 1/4 cup biscuit baking mix
1 cup nuts, chopped
1/2 cup (4-ounce jar) chopped maraschino cherries, drained
1 cup dates, cut up

Mix margarine, sugar and eggs. Stir in baking mix. Fold in nuts, cherries and dates. Spread dough in greased pan 9x13-inch pan and bake at 375 degrees for 30 minutes. Cool slightly. Cut into 1 1/2-inch squares.

Yield: 48 squares

Priscilla Davidson
Washington

Old-Fashioned Butter Cookies

1	cup sugar
1	egg
1	cup sweet cream butter, softened
2 1/2	cups all-purpose flour
1	teaspoon baking powder
2	tablespoons orange juice
1	teaspoon vanilla
	Frosting

Cream butter, sugar and egg until light and fluffy. Beat in flour, baking powder, orange juice and vanilla until smooth. Chill 2 to 3 hours. Preheat oven to 400 degrees. Working with half the dough at a time, roll out on lightly floured surface to 1/8 to 1/4 inch thickness. Cut into desired shapes. Bake on ungreased cookie sheet 6 to 10 minutes, or until edges are golden brown. Cool on racks.

Yield: 6 dozen 2-inch cookies.

These cookies are delicious plain or iced with the following frosting.

Frosting

3	cups confectioners' sugar
1/3	cup butter, softened
1 to 2	tablespoons milk
1	teaspoon vanilla

In medium bowl, cream sugar and butter together at low speed. Add milk and vanilla. Beat until fluffy. Add food coloring, if desired.

Note: You may substitute almond extract for the vanilla for a rich flavor.

Laura T. Smithwick
Washington

Baby Ruth Bars

4   cups oatmeal
1   cup brown sugar
1/4   cup white corn syrup
1/4   cup crunchy peanut butter
1 or 2 drops almond flavoring
2/3   cup margarine or butter, melted

Preheat oven to 400 degrees. Grease 9x13-inch pan.

Mix above ingredients, and spread and pack down into prepared pan. Bake for 10 minutes. While cooling, prepare the following topping.

Topping

1   (6-ounce) package chocolate chips
1/2   (6-ounce) package butterscotch chips
3/4   cup crunchy peanut butter

Melt above together. Spread over baked layer. Cover with foil and chill. Freezes well.

Yield: 48 squares

Frances Stephenson
Washington

Peanut Butter Slices

1   (11-ounce) bag butterscotch chips
1   cup peanut butter
1/2   cup coconut
1/2   cup chopped nuts
1   package miniature marshmallows

Melt the chips and peanut butter. Let the mixture cool. Add coconut, nuts and marshmallows. Mix well. Press mixture into a 9x13-inch pan and refrigerate.

Peggy Mers
Aurora

I make these for Christmas.

Chocolate Amaretto Balls

3	(6-ounce) packages semi-sweet chocolate chips
1	(14-ounce) can sweetened condensed milk
3	tablespoons amaretto liqueur
1/2	teaspoon almond extract
	finely chopped almonds

This is a great giveaway at Christmas. Your mailman will love you! Get the amaretto from the liquor store when nobody's looking!

Over low heat, melt chocolate chips with condensed milk. Remove from heat and stir in amaretto and almond extract. Chill two hours. Shape into 3/4 inch balls and roll in almonds. Chill until firm. Store at room temperature in a tightly covered container. Flavor improves after 24 hours.

Variation: omit amaretto, almond extract, and almonds. Instead, stir 1/2 cup dark rum into melted chocolate mixture. Chill, shape, and roll in flaked coconut.

Jan De Hoog
Terra Ceia

Fruit Bars

1	cup water
1	cup raisins
1	apple, peeled and chopped
1/4	cup shortening
2	tablespoons liquid sweetener
1	teaspoon cinnamon
1/4	teaspoon nutmeg
1	egg
1	teaspoon vanilla
1/2	teaspoon black walnut flavoring or 1/2 cup chopped walnuts
1	cup all-purpose flour
1	teaspoon baking soda
1/4	teaspoon salt

Combine water, raisins, apple, shortening, sweetener, cinnamon and nutmeg. Boil 3 minutes. Cool. Beat egg, add vanilla and walnut flavorings (or chopped walnuts). Add flour, baking soda and salt. Stir the two mixtures together. Spread in 9x9-inch pan. Bake at 350 degrees for 25 minutes.

Yield: 25 bars

Flo Meier
Washington

Esther Keyzer's Dutch Bitter Koekjes (Almond Macaroons)

1 pound almond paste
4 egg whites
1 cup sugar
2 cups confectioners' sugar

Work the almond paste with one egg white until lumps are gone. Add granulated sugar and another egg white. Work until smooth. Add remaining egg whites and confectioners' sugar and mix well. Line cookie sheets with aluminum foil. Drop dough by tablespoons on the foil. Bake at 325 degrees for 20 minutes. Cool on foil before removing cookies. Macaroons freeze well.

Note: Almond paste is available at the Terra Ceia Christian School.

Corry T. Harris
Pantego

Flossie Ricks of Pantego, catering Sunday dinners, served food from the mid-40s to the late 60s in her home, which became known as "Flossie's House."

Mom-Mom's Swedish Cookies

1 1/2 cups melted shortening or 3 sticks softened margarine
2 eggs
1 cup sugar
1 cup brown sugar
1 teaspoon baking soda in 2 teaspoons boiling water
4 cups all-purpose flour
1 teaspoon salt
1 cup chopped nuts

Cream shortening or margarine with sugar, eggs, and soda mixture. Add dry ingredients one cup at a time, mixing well after each addition. Make a compact roll and wrap in wax paper. Lay roll flat in cake pan and let it stand overnight. Slice as thinly as possible, keeping the dough very cold until cut. Bake at 350 degrees until light brown.

Yield: 10 dozen.

Elenore Van Essendelft
Terra Ceia

This is a favorite recipe which came from Long Island, but was brought to eastern Beaufort County during the late 1970s.

Toffee Bars

1/2	cup butter
1/2	cup brown sugar
1	cup all-purpose flour
1/2	teaspoon vanilla
5	milk chocolate bars
	chopped pecans

Soften butter and mix with brown sugar, vanilla and flour. Mix these well and press into a 9x9-inch baking pan. Bake at 350 degrees for 15 minutes. Remove pan and while hot, place chocolate bars on top of batter. Once the chocolate bars melt, swirl them, smooth evenly and sprinkle the pecans over chocolate. Let cool and cut into bars.

Yield: 16 cookies

Sarah Sloan
Washington

Town House Delights

These crackers are easy and fast, and they also go fast wherever I carry them.

8	ounces chopped dates
1	can sweetened condensed milk
1	cup chopped pecans
	Town House crackers

Cook dates and milk until thick over medium heat, stirring constantly. Add pecans. Spread over Town House crackers. Bake at 350 degrees for 8 minutes.

Icing

3	ounces cream cheese
1/4	cup margarine
1	teaspoon vanilla
2	cups confectioners' sugar

Beat first 3 ingredients until smooth. Gradually add sugar; spread over cooled cookies.

Yield: 50 or more cookies.

Christine Jackson
Pinetown

Pecan Snaps

1/4   cup packed brown sugar
1/4   cup margarine or butter
1/4   cup maple syrup
1/2   cup finely ground pecans
1/3   cup all-purpose flour
1   tablespoon brandy or 1 teaspoon vanilla

In a small saucepan combine brown sugar, margarine or butter, and maple syrup. Cook and stir over medium heat till the sugar is dissolved and the margarine is melted. Remove from heat. Stir in pecans, flour, and brandy or vanilla.

Line a cookie sheet with foil; lightly grease the foil with margarine or butter. Drop the batter from a level teaspoon about 5 inches apart onto the cookie sheet. (Only bake 4 or 5 cookies at a time because you need to shape them quickly before they harden.) Bake at 350 degrees for 8 to 10 minutes or till bubbly and deep golden brown.

Remove from oven and let stand on cookie sheet on wire rack for 1 minute. Immediately remove cookies from foil, flipping with a spatula onto the counter. With flat side to the inside, roll cookies around the greased handle of a wooden spoon, letting the bowl of the spoon hang over the edge of the counter. Remove the wooden spoon, keeping the rolled shape.

Cool on a wire rack, (If cookies harden before you can shape them, return them to the hot oven for 1 minute or until softened.) Repeat with remaining batter.

Yield: 3 dozen cookies

Pamela Gunnin Burkart
Washington

Make these crispy, rolled wafers ahead and store them between layers of wax paper in a covered container. You can freeze them to up to 12 months.

These are a little trouble to fix, but worth it. I try to bake them when no one is at home ... otherwise, we eat them then and there, never having enough to save. They are great served with a bowl of ice cream, also. They dress up the dish and the crunchy, nutty taste is wonderful.

Peanut Brittle

1/4   teaspoon nutmeg
1/2   teaspoon salt, scant
1   teaspoon soda, heaping
1 1/2 cup sugar
1/2   cup dark corn syrup
1/2   cup water
2   cups peanuts

Mix nutmeg, salt and soda and set aside. Cook sugar, syrup and water to boiling point. Add peanuts and cook, stirring occasionally to 300 degrees. Remove from heat and stir in dry mixture thoroughly, but fast. Pour out onto greased marble. Push up around sides with knife or hands. When cool enough to break into pieces.

Jane Hodges
Washington

This is an old Washington recipe.

You Can't Believe It's Not Toffee

1   cup butter
1   cup brown sugar
     Waverly crackers
     milk chocolate morsels

Combine butter and brown sugar and cook over medium heat until it foams. This will take a while. Line cookie sheet with aluminum foil. Place Waverly crackers over foil making a solid base. Pour butter and sugar mix over crackers and spread with metal spoon. Place in 350 degree oven until it bubbles. Remove from oven and sprinkle a 12-ounce package of milk chocolate morsels over crackers and spread with metal spoon. Refrigerate until it hardens and break into pieces.

Note: May use white chocolate and may also add nuts. Graham crackers may be substituted for Waverly crackers.

Jaye Jenkins
Washington

BG's Fudge

2   cups sugar
1/2   cup milk
3   squares unsweetened chocolate
4   tablespoons butter, divided
1   tablespoon dark corn syrup
         pinch of salt
1   teaspoon vanilla
3/4 to 1 cup nuts (pecans or if black walnuts, use less)

My mother always made the best fudge, which is a variation of her mother's famous fudge. Of course she didn't really measure anything, and when I asked for the recipe, she used terms like, "hunk" of butter. You won't be able to make it as good as she, but you can try.

Grease a pan or plate with 2 tablespoons butter. Stir sugar, milk, chocolate, 2 tablespoons butter, corn syrup and salt until melted. Continue to stir until mixture is at soft ball stage. (Spoon a tiny amount into a cup of water; if it forms a ball, it's ready.) Fill the sink with a couple of inches of water and put the pot in it to cool the chocolate mixture. Add the remaining butter and vanilla. Beat with an electric mixer before it gets too cool, then quickly fold in the nuts. Spread on the greased plate. If it gets too hard, add a little milk and heat up again. Timing is important.

Katherine Howdy Tate
Washington

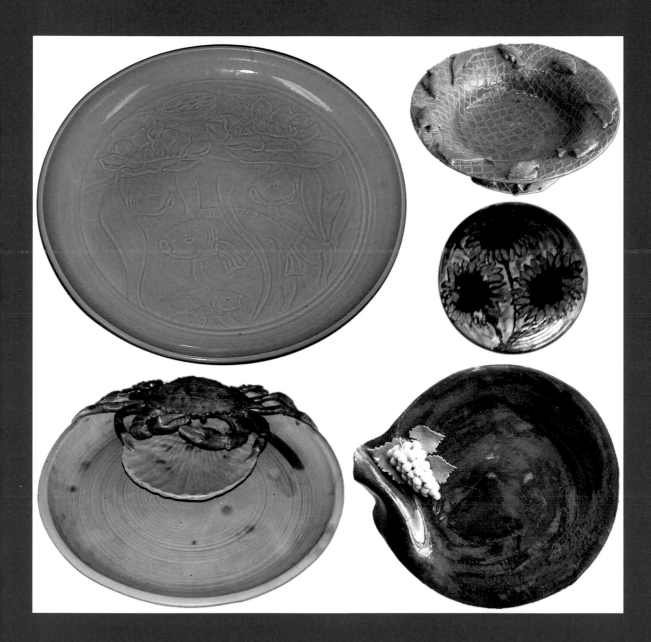

Irene Forbes
Diane Lee
Lyn Mallison Morrow
Roberta Woolridge

ceramics

Mixed Media

Oyster Gravy

1/4	cup finely chopped onion
2	tablespoons oil
2	tablespoons all-purpose flour
1	cup water
1/8	teaspoon pepper
1/4	teaspoon salt
1	dozen oysters with juice

Sauté onions in oil. Add flour and blend into oil, making a light brown roux. Add water and stir until thickened. Season with the salt and pepper. Add oysters with juice and cook until the oysters begin to curl. Serve hot over split biscuits or English muffins.

Yield: 4 servings

Dr. Tom Phillips
Former resident, Washington

An old cookbook revealed that George Washington enjoyed Oyster Gravy (with a touch of mace) poured over warm Virginia ham slices – try it!

Tomato Gravy

	drippings from 4 strips of bacon
2	(16-ounce) cans tomatoes, drained and chopped
1/4	cup all-purpose flour
1	cup milk
	Tabasco sauce, to taste
	salt, to taste
	pepper, to taste

In a large skillet, heat the bacon fat. Add well-chopped tomatoes and sauté, stirring often, for 30 minutes or until tomatoes are mush. Slowly add milk and flour, stirring constantly until the mixture thickens. Stir in salt, pepper and Tabasco sauce. Add a little bit of milk to mix and stir well. Serve over fresh biscuits.

Note: You can substitute butter for bacon grease.

Yield: 4 servings

Carol Nash
Washington Park

Try this gravy over cooked grits. Break into bits the bacon you fried for bacon grease and sprinkle on top of the gravy. Very tasty!

Cheese Marinated Onions

3	ounces blue cheese, crumbled
1/2	cup salad oil
2	tablespoons lemon juice
1	teaspoon Nature's Seasons (or salt)
1/2	teaspoon sugar
	dash of paprika
4	medium onions, sliced thin (or 4 cups onion rings)

Mix all ingredients except onion rings. Pour over onion rings and refrigerate 3 to 4 hours. Shake occasionally.

Yield: 8 cups

Frances Larkin
Washington Park

Cheese Strata

Barbara Gray Howdy gave this to me at book club.

Try the Tomato Gravy with this - great!

8	slices bread, crusts removed
	butter
1/2 to 3/4	pound sharp cheddar, grated
3 to 4	eggs, beaten
2 1/2	cups milk, whole or skim
1	teaspoon salt
1 1/2	teaspoons dry mustard

Butter bread lightly on both sides and quarter the slices. Mix together cheese, eggs, milk, salt and mustard. In a greased 9x13-inch glass baking dish, put bread on the bottom and pour milk mixture on top of bread. Let stand 2 hours or freeze. Bake at 350 degrees for 1 hour, until bubbly and brown. Can be a breakfast meal with layer of cooked sausage or ham in the middle.

Yield: 6 servings

Ramona Cayton
Washington

That Wonderful Horseradish Mold!

1   package lemon flavored gelatin
1   envelope unflavored gelatin
1   (8-ounce) jar hot horseradish
1   cup mayonnaise
1   (16-ounce) container sour cream

This is a great side dish with pork loin roast or ham.

Dissolve lemon gelatin in 1/2 cup boiling water. Dissolve unflavored gelatin in 2 tablespoons cold water. Mix gelatins. Add all other ingredients and blend with whisk. Lightly oil a cold mold and pour ingredients into it. (I use my Bundt pan.)

Yield: 12 to 14 servings

Nannelle Smyre
Chocowinity

Barbecue Marinade/Sauce

1   teaspoon black pepper
1   teaspoon cayenne pepper
1/4   cup Worcestershire sauce
1/4   cup Heinz 57 Sauce
       water

Use as a cooking liquid for pork (roasts, chops, ribs). Use as a marinade and basting liquid for grilling or baking chicken or pork.

Combine seasoning and sauces in a 4-cup measuring cup. Fill cup to 4-cup level with water. Stir to combine all ingredients.

Note: Spiciness can be adjusted by increasing ingredient amount or by diluting recipe.

Ann Peters
Washington

Richard's Barbecue Sauce

1   cup ketchup
2   tablespoons vinegar
2   tablespoons honey
1   tablespoon prepared mustard
1   teaspoon Kitchen Bouquet (optional)
       a little finely chopped onion (optional)

Combine all ingredients and mix thoroughly. Spoon or brush the sauce over chicken, beef or pork and refrigerate over night if possible. Bake meats at 325 degrees, if not grilling, until done. If needed, lightly cover with foil so sauce will not burn.

Evelyn L. Tripp
Washington

Tim's Chicken Barbecue Sauce

2	cups wine vinegar (red with garlic or white with tarragon works best)
1	cup water
1	stick margarine
1/2	cup Worcestershire sauce
2	tablespoons soy sauce
1	medium onion, chopped
2	garlic cloves, finely chopped
1/4	cup brown sugar
1	lemon, juiced with whole peel
1	teaspoon Tabasco sauce
1/2	teaspoon cayenne pepper
2	teaspoons black pepper
1	tablespoon salt
1	teaspoon ground oregano
1	bay leaf

Combine all ingredients and slowly bring to a boil. Keep warm as you baste chicken.

Yield: approximately 1 quart

Emily M. Ashburn
Washington

Shrimp Sauce

1/2	onion, grated
1	pint mayonnaise
1	teaspoon Worcestershire sauce
1/2	teaspoon Tabasco sauce
1	teaspoon curry powder
2	tablespoons horseradish
2	tablespoons ketchup
5	tablespoons chili sauce
1	teaspoon salt
	freshly ground pepper, to taste

Combine all ingredients and mix well.

Beth Sloan
Washington

Salsa Verde (Green Salsa)

4	large jalapeño peppers, whole
8 to 10	tomatillos, green tomatoes with leaf covering
1	teaspoon salt
1/2 to 3/4	teaspoon garlic powder

Boil peppers and tomatillos in medium saucepan until the centers are done. Place peppers and tomatilloes in blender and add remaining ingredients; purée until well mixed. May be refrigerated in closed container for 7 to 10 days.

Dannielle Valdez
Chocowinity

Jalapeño peppers and tomatillos are found in the produce section of your favorite store.

Salsa Rojo (Red Salsa)

4 to 5	red dried serrano peppers
2	whole red tomatoes
1	teaspoon salt
1/2 to 3/4	teaspoon garlic powder

Boil peppers and tomatoes in medium saucepan until the red peppers are soft. Place peppers and tomatoes in blender and add remaining ingredients. Purée until well mixed. May be refrigerated in closed container for 7 to 10 days.

Dannielle Valdez
Chocowinity

Blue Cheese Dressing

3/4	cup milk (or less)
1	(8-ounce) package cream cheese, softened and cut up
1	(4-ounce) package blue cheese, crumbled
1/2	teaspoon tarragon
1/4	teaspoon pepper
	small clove garlic
1/2	teaspoon salt (or less)

Put all ingredients in a food processor and blend until smooth.

Frank Bonner
Aurora

Miss Myrtle Rowe's Restaurant in Aurora was considered "the best place to eat" during the 40s and 50s.

Lewessar Salad Dressing

This is the best dressing I have ever had. I know you will love it too.

1	cup fresh lemon juice
1	teaspoon salt
1/2	teaspoon powdered ginger
1/4	teaspoon celery salt
1/8	teaspoon garlic salt
1/4	teaspoon dry mustard
1/4	teaspoon onion salt
1/4	teaspoon paprika
1/2	teaspoon Accent
2	tablespoons chili sauce
6	tablespoons sugar
1	cup vegetable oil

Put all ingredients except oil in a glass jar and shake until sugar is dissolved. This is VERY important. Add the oil, close jar tightly. Shake until blended. Chill well before using. Keep refrigerated.

Laura Bell
Washington Park

Egg Brunch

This may be prepared the day before, refrigerated and heated before serving.

4	slices bacon, cut up
1/2	pound dried beef, cut coarsely
2	(3-ounce) cans sliced mushrooms, drained
1/2	cup butter, divided
1/2	cup all-purpose flour
1	quart milk
	pepper, to taste
1/4	teaspoon salt
16	eggs
1	cup evaporated milk

To make sauce: Sauté bacon until almost done. Pour off grease. Add dried beef, mushrooms and 1/4 cup butter. While still hot, add flour, milk and pepper (but no salt). Stir until thickened and smooth. In a large bowl, mix eggs with salt and evaporated milk. Scramble in 1/4 cup butter. Butter a 3-quart casserole. Place small amount of bacon/mushroom sauce in bottom, then a layer of eggs, layer of sauce, another layer of eggs and top with sauce. Garnish the top with mushrooms, if desired. Cover and bake at 275 degrees for one hour.

Yield: 10 to 12 servings

Beth Page
Washington

The Best Country Ham and Egg Quiche

Wonderful for brunches and luncheons!

Crust

2   cups all-purpose flour
1   teaspoon baking powder
1/2   teaspoon salt
1/2   cup milk
1/3   cup cooking oil

Preheat oven to 350 degrees. In a mixing bowl, stir together flour, salt and baking powder. Make a well in the center. Combine oil and milk and pour into dry mixture. Stir until moistened. Turn onto floured surface and knead a short time until smooth. Roll into a 12-inch circle. Lay in pie pan. Crimp edges.

Filling

6   eggs, beaten slightly
1   cup cottage cheese
1/2   cup shredded mozzarella cheese
1/2   cup shredded sharp cheddar cheese
1/4   cup chopped country ham
1/4   cup chopped hard salami
2   tablespoons sliced green onion
2   tablespoons chopped fresh parsley

In another bowl, mix filling ingredients. Pour into unbaked crust. Bake for 50 to 55 minutes, or until knife inserted in center comes out clean. Let stand for 10 minutes before serving.

Yield: 8 servings

Margaret Sloan Trainer
Washington

Pesto with Spicy Basil

2	cups basil leaves, firmly packed
2	tablespoons pine nuts or chopped walnuts
1/2	cup olive oil
1/2	cup grated Parmesan or Romano cheese
	salt and fresh ground pepper, as desired

Put all ingredients except cheese into a blender and blend at high speed until the sauce has the consistency of whipped butter. Push the basil leaves down from time to time and add a little more olive oil if the contents stick. Add grated cheese and toss in a large bowl with enough spaghetti for four main dish servings. This is excellent served with slices of fried or broiled meat, chicken or fish, or with baked eggplant for a vegetarian entrée.

Yield: 4 servings

Vera Van Camp
Washington

Herb Mixtures for Roasts

Use herbs with a light touch until you discover what tastes best to you.

Remember: Dried herbs are more potent than fresh ones, so adjust your recipe accordingly.

Two basic herb mixtures are:

• Fines Herbes - a mixture of fresh parsley, chives, tarragon and chervil (optional)

• Bouquet Garni - 2 sprigs fresh thyme, 4 to 6 sprigs fresh parsley, 1 bay leaf tied together with string.

Or, if dried, use 1/4 teaspoon crushed thyme, 1 tablespoon chopped parsley, and 1 broken bay leaf tied together in a square of cheesecloth.

Here are some great herb mixtures for out-of-this-world roasts. The easiest way to mince fresh herbs is to use a pair of scissors and snip the leaves while they're still attached to the stems. When using herb mixtures, cut slits in the meat with a sharp paring knife and force a little of the mixture into each slit, using equal amounts of each herb.

HERB MIXTURE FOR LEG OF LAMB ROAST: Marjoram, rosemary, summer savory, parsley, chervil.

HERB MIXTURE FOR BEEF ROAST: Savory, basil marjoram, parsley, chervil.

HERB MIXTURE FOR PORK ROAST: Savory, spicy basil, sage, rosemary.

Here is an old-world suggestion for roasting meat that will enhance the delicious flavors of your herbs. Encase the meat in a brown paper bag in a medium hot oven for the usual time until done to your liking.

Vera Van Camp
Washington

Fruit Crumble Topping

3/4 cup brown sugar, packed
2 cups biscuit baking mix
1 1/2 cups quick oatmeal
1/2 cup margarine or butter, softened

Mix dry ingredients and cut in margarine until it is in fine pieces. Store in refrigerator. When ready to use, pour desired amount of any canned pie filling or fruit into greased oven dish. When using fresh fruit, add 2 teaspoons cornstarch or 4 teaspoons flour to juice to thicken. Sprinkle with topping. Bake at 350 degrees for 25 minutes.

Helen Myers
Pantego

I usually prepare a double batch to have on hand for a quick dessert.

Apple, Mint Leaf and Orange Relish

1 unpeeled orange
1 cup applesauce
1/2 cup fresh mint leaves, chopped

Grate the orange rind, chop the orange pulp and combine these with the remaining ingredients. Marinate for several hours before serving. Use with lamb, ham or turkey.

Vera Van Camp
Washington

Frozen Cranberry Relish

Great with pork and beef - a family favorite (and no, it's not gelatin salad!)

2	cups fresh cranberries
1	small onion, cut into fourths
1/2	cup sugar
3/4	cup sour cream
2	tablespoons prepared horseradish

Process the cranberries and onion in a food processor, chopped but not puréed. In a bowl, combine sugar, sour cream and horseradish. Stir in cranberries and onion. Pour into a 9-inch square pan, pat down and freeze. Remove from freezer one hour prior to serving. Spoon mixture into a serving bowl and chop up. (It will still be partially frozen.)

Anne Stuart Rumley
Washington

Brandied Fig/Strawberry Jam

5	cups fig chunks
2	cups quartered strawberries
5	cups sugar
5	tablespoons brandy (divided)
1	tablespoon whole crushed allspice or 2 teaspoons ground allspice
1	lemon, juice and zest
1	tablespoon pure vanilla extract

Combine and crush fruit lightly. Place in large stainless steel or enamel pot. Stir in sugar until dissolved. Add 3 tablespoons brandy and allspice. Simmer and stir to prevent sticking until jelly stage is reached. (Jam will sheet off a cold metal spoon and break away.) Remove from heat and add 2 tablespoons brandy and the vanilla. Fill sterilized jelly jars. Process in hot water bath 10 minutes.

Yield: 8 half-pints

Recipe developed by
Irene Forbes
Washington

and Linda C. Miller
Blount's Creek

Riley Potts Simpson

Mr. Bear Comes to Breakfast

mixed media

Children's Creations

Caramel Apple Smoothie

1   cup vanilla ice cream
3/4   cup apple juice
1 1/2 cups peeled and chopped Granny Smith apples
1   tablespoon fresh lemon juice
3   tablespoons caramel sauce

Put ingredients into a blender and blend until smooth.

Yield: 2 servings

Tastes like caramel apples from the fair. This one is in a glass, not on a stick.

Easy. Smaller children should have adult supervision.

Tatum Edwards
Washington

Yogoreo Shake

2   cups milk
4   cups frozen vanilla yogurt
1/2   teaspoon vanilla
I   dozen oreos, crushed

Put cookies in a plastic bag and pound until cookies are crushed. Combine milk, frozen yogurt and vanilla in a blender and mix until creamy. Add cookies to yogurt mixture and blend until mixed thoroughly.

Yield: 4 servings

A milkshake full of cookies! What more could you ask?

Smaller children should have adult supervision.

Lewis Sloan, Jr.
Washington

Jungle Shake

2   bananas, cut up
1/2   cup milk
1   cup vanilla ice cream
1   tablespoon peanut butter

Pour milk in the blender. Add bananas, ice cream and peanut butter. Blend for 10 seconds. This makes a delicious shake.

Yield: 2 servings

Sure to tame the wild animals in your home.

Jay Campbell
Washington

Janie's Apple Dip

Fun to take on a picnic or out on the river!

1	(8-ounce) package cream cheese
1/2	teaspoon vanilla
1	cup peanuts, crushed
3/4	cup brown sugar
	apples
	processed cheese slices

Blend cream cheese, vanilla, peanuts and brown sugar, well. Core half an apple and fill with dip. Cut a sail out of cheese, thread it onto a toothpick and stick it into the "boat." Place the boat on a plate and surround with apple slices for dipping.

Janie Page
Washington

Harvest Dip for Apples

A taste of Fall, all year!

1	(8-ounce) carton sour cream
1	tablespoon sugar
1/2	teaspoon pumpkin pie spice
1/4	teaspoon vanilla
4	medium apples

Combine sour cream, sugar, pumpkin pie spice and vanilla. Chill covered, until ready to serve. Cut apples into wedges for dipping.

Yield: 1 cup

Reed Padgett
Washington

Christmas Crunch Mix

6	cups popped popcorn
4	cups Honey Nut Chex cereal
1	(7-ounce) jar marshmallow creme
20	red or green hard peppermint candies, crushed (1/2 cup)

Preheat oven to 350 degrees. Spray cookie sheet with cooking spray. Mix popcorn and cereal in large bowl. Set aside. Place marshmallow creme in medium microwavable bowl. Microwave uncovered on high about 2 minutes, stirring after 1 minute, until melted. Stir again. Pour over popcorn mixture. Stir until evenly coated. Sprinkle with candies. Spread mixture on cookie sheet. Bake 5 minutes; stir. Bake about 5 minutes longer, or until coating is light golden brown. Spread on waxed paper or aluminum foil to cool. Store tightly covered.

Yield: about 20 (1/2 cup) servings

Sarah Jennings
Washington

Crunchy Citrus Spice Mix

1	(6-ounce) package Bugles original flavor snacks
1	(12-ounce) can mixed nuts or peanuts
2	egg whites
2	tablespoons orange juice or water
1 1/3	cups sugar
2	teaspoons ground cinnamon
1	cup dried cranberries or cherries

A refreshing new twist for snack mix!

Preheat oven to 275 degrees. Grease jelly roll pan (10x15-inch). Mix Bugles and nuts in large bowl. Beat egg whites, orange juice, sugar and cinnamon in small bowl, using wire whisk or hand beater until foamy. Pour over snack mixture; stir until evenly coated. Spread in pan. Bake uncovered for 35 minutes, stirring every 15 minutes, or until light brown and crisp. Cool completely. Store in airtight container.

Yield: 20 servings (1/2 cup each)

John Tate
Washington

Chili Popcorn

This is a nice twist to the same old popcorn. The kids will love this!

3   tablespoons butter, melted
1 1/2 teaspoons chili powder
1/2   teaspoon salt
1/2   teaspoon garlic powder
1/2   teaspoon paprika
12   cups freshly popped popcorn

Combine first 5 ingredients. Drizzle over warm popcorn, stirring to coat.

Yield: 12 servings

Gray, Madison and Sam Murray
Washington

All-American Popcorn

       melted butter
2   quarts popped corn
       seasoned salt
       grated American cheese
       dry onion soup mix
       bacon flavored bits

Drizzle butter over popped corn and add seasoned salt, cheese, soup mix and bacon bits.

Yield: 8 servings

William Tate
Washington

Reese Cup Popcorn

2   tablespoons butter or margarine
1   tablespoon cream or chunky peanut butter
2   quarts popped corn
1   (16-ounce) bag milk chocolate chips

Melt butter with peanut butter in small saucepan, blending until smooth. Pour over popped corn, mix well. Add chocolate chips, stir and season to taste with salt.

Yield: 8 servings

Daniel May
Washington

Red Devil

1	can tomato soup, undiluted
1	heaping teaspoon mustard
	dash of Worcestershire sauce
	dash of Tabasco sauce
1	cup sharp cheddar cheese, shredded

Combine the first 4 ingredients in a saucepan. Cook over medium heat until bubbly. Add cheese and stir constantly until cheese is almost melted. Pour over saltine crackers or dip crackers into the Red Devil.

Yield: 4 servings

Hawes and Beck Collier
Washington

An old recipe from their great grandmother, Martha Hardy Hodges. It's quick and easy.

Clark Brothers' Pizza Quesadillas

flour tortillas
cheddar cheese, grated
pepperoni, thinly sliced (get pre-sliced)

Place one flour tortilla in a frying pan on low heat (no oil). Spread cheese on tortilla and layer on pepperoni. Top off with a second flour tortilla and cover pan with lid for one minute. Remove the lid and flip the "sandwich" and replace the lid for another minute. When the cheese is melted, cut the pizza into wedges.

This is so easy, especially if you buy shredded cheese and pre-sliced pepperoni. Easy to clean up and delicious for the kids.

Alex and Tyler Clark
Washington

Variations: Leave out pepperoni and substitute whatever your child prefers. Cut into smaller slices and provide sauces for dipping (marinara, ranch and salsa are good ideas.) Tortillas burn easily so watch closely and keep the heat low.

Layered Mexican Pizza

1	(16-ounce) can refried beans
1	(10-ounce) can chicken (in water), drained and separated
1	(12-ounce) package 4-cheese Mexican blend
3	10-inch flour tortillas
2/3	cup salsa

Eat and enjoy! Goes great with sour cream and guacamole!

Spray a round, 10-inch microwavable glass container with cooking spray. Place one tortilla in dish, layer half of beans and half of chicken; pour salsa evenly over chicken. Sprinkle half of cheese on salsa and top with another tortilla. Repeat the process, ending with a tortilla on top. Put in microwave for 5 minutes and turn if necessary. You may have to adjust the cooking time, depending on your microwave; you be the judge.

Yield: 2 servings

Etta Buckman
Washington

Fun French Toast

6	eggs
1	teaspoon sugar
2	teaspoons milk
12	pieces of Texas Toast bread or regular loaf bread
	cinnamon
	peanut butter
	syrup

Every Sunday morning Daniel and A.J. wake me up so that we can make our "special family breakfast." They enjoy helping out in the kitchen as long as they don't have to wash the dishes.

Adult supervision. Easy.

Mix eggs, sugar and milk together in a large bowl. Heat lightly greased pan on medium until hot. Dip bread into egg mixture and place in pan. Lightly sprinkle cinnamon on top side of bread. When bread is brown on the bottom, turn it over and lightly sprinkle with cinnamon. After toast has finished cooking, spread desired amount of peanut butter over top piece of toast and add syrup to taste.

Please note: If you have a peanut allergy, peanut butter can be eliminated.

Yield: 3 to 4 servings

Daniel and A.J. Valdez
Chocowinity

Breakfast Sandwich

1/4   medium banana, peeled
2   teaspoons peanut butter
2   frozen pancakes, thawed
6   miniature marshmallows
6   chocolate chips

Adult supervision. Easy.

Slice banana into thin slices. Spread 1 teaspoon peanut butter on each pancake. Place sliced bananas, marshmallows and chocolate chips on top of peanut butter on 1 pancake. Next, place other pancake, peanut butter side down, on top of first pancake and press down gently. Put on paper plate. Microwave on high for 1 minute, or until chocolate chips and marshmallows are melted. Carefully remove plate from microwave. Serve warm.

Yield: 1 sandwich

Jay Campbell
Washington

Easy Chicken Tenders

1/2   cup cornflakes cereal
1 1/2   tablespoons all-purpose flour
1/2   teaspoon paprika
1/4   teaspoon onion powder
    pinch of ground sage
    salt and pepper
1/4   cup milk
1   package chicken, boneless strips

Serve with honey mustard dressing or barbeque sauce for dipping.

Preheat oven to 350 degrees. Crush cornflakes in a large zip top plastic bag. Add flour, paprika, onion powder, sage, salt and pepper to crushed cornflakes. Seal bag and shake. Pour milk into bowl. Rinse chicken and pat dry. Dip each chicken piece into milk and one at a time, put chicken strips into bag of cornflakes, and shake. When chicken is completely covered with flakes, place on a baking sheet. Bake for approximately 20 minutes, or until done.

Tatum Edwards
Washington

Honey Mustard Dressing

3/4   cup mayonnaise
1/4   cup honey
3   tablespoons Dijon mustard
1   teaspoon vinegar
1/4   teaspoon salt

Whisk ingredients until combined. Keeps in refrigerator up to a week.

Yield: 1 cup

Tori Edwards
Washington

Lewis' Secret Sauce

1/4   cup dill pickle juice
1/4   cup ketchup
1/4   cup mustard
2   tablespoons ranch dressing
1   cup mayonnaise
       several shakes black pepper

Great on burgers! Easy. Will keep for one week.

Pour pickle juice into a glass bowl. Whisk in other ingredients until blended. Refrigerate unused portion.

Yield: approximately 2 cups

Lewis Sloan, Jr.
Washington

Lasagna Roll-Ups

8	ounces cooked lasagna noodles (about 1/2 box)
2	cups ricotta cheese
1	cup grated mozzarella cheese
2	eggs, lightly beaten
1	jar spaghetti sauce

Preheat oven to 350 degrees. Pour half the sauce over the bottom of a medium sized baking dish. Mix ricotta cheese, mozzarella cheese and eggs in a bowl. Lay a lasagna noodle on a flat surface and with a spatula, spread some of the cheese mixture on the noodle. (Leave a little room at the ends and on the sides so that the cheese won't ooze out when you roll up the noodles.) Roll up noodle and place it, edge down, in the dish. After you've rolled up all the noodles, pour the remaining spaghetti sauce all over the top of them. Bake in the oven for about 15 minutes. Serve hot.

Yield: 4 servings

Carly Phillips
Washington

Flaky Cut-Outs

1	pound margarine
1/2	cup shortening
3	eggs
1	cup sugar
1	teaspoon flavoring (vanilla, anise, etc.)
	pinch of salt
2	teaspoons baking powder
5 1/2 to 6	cups all-purpose flour

Preheat oven to 375 degrees. Cream together margarine, shortening and eggs. Add sugar, flavoring, salt, baking powder and flour. Mix and roll out, then cut. Bake for 8 to 10 minutes on greased baking sheets. Frost cookies with Confectioners' Sugar Icing or Easy Royal Icing (recipes follow).

Note: You may want to chill dough before cutting.

Davis Lane Rumley
Washington

Kids love these cookies because they are soft and flaky, unlike sugar cookies that harden after baking.

Confectioners' Sugar Icing

2   sticks butter or margarine
1   pound confectioners' sugar
1   teaspoon vanilla
    milk

Cream butter, sugar and vanilla, adding milk to reach a spreadable consistency. Color as desired.

Davis Lane Rumley
Washington

Easy Royal Icing

1   (16-ounce) can prepared frosting
    food coloring

Place frosting in microwave-safe measuring cup with pouring spout. Microwave until pourable. DO NOT BOIL. Stir in desired food coloring. Pour frosting over cookie and let sit approximately 10 minutes. Reheat frosting as needed to keep it pourable.

Davis Lane Rumley
Washington

No Bake Cookies

4   cups of sugar
1   cup of milk
1   cup of cocoa
1/4   teaspoon of salt
1   cup of peanut butter
1   cup of margarine
6   cups of oatmeal

Adult supervision needed until mixture is removed from heat.

Combine sugar, milk, cocoa, margarine and salt in a pan over medium heat. Bring this mixture to a boil, stirring constantly. Once the mixture boils, remove from the heat and add the peanut butter and oatmeal. Drop by spoonfuls onto waxed paper.

Yield: 5 dozen cookies

Tori Edwards
Washington

Buckeye Balls

1   (16-ounce) jar creamy peanut butter
1   cup butter or margarine, softened
1 1/2 pounds confectioners' sugar
2   cups semisweet chocolate morsels
2   tablespoons shortening

Beat peanut butter and butter at medium speed with an electric mixer until blended. Gradually add confectioners' sugar, beating until blended. Shape into 1-inch balls; chill 10 minutes or until firm. Microwave chocolate and shortening in a 2-quart glass bowl on high 1 1/2 minutes or until melted, stirring twice. Dip each ball in chocolate mixture until partially coated; place on wax paper to harden. Store in an airtight container.

Yield: 7 dozen

Marella and Ben Peele
Bath

These are unbelievably good - great to have at home for the holidays or to give as gifts.

"Mudder's" Cherry Pie

2   pie crusts (regular size, not deep dish)
1   pound can red tart pitted cherries, packed in water (2 cups) - do not use pie filling
2/3 cup sugar
2   tablespoons cornstarch
1/4 teaspoon salt
1   teaspoon cinnamon
2   tablespoons butter (maybe more)

Drain liquid from the cherries and heat in a saucepan. Mix the 4 dry ingredients. Sift into the boiling liquid. Cook until thick and clear, stirring constantly. Add butter and cherries and pour into unbaked 8-inch pie shell. Cover with top crust. Bake in moderately hot oven (350 degrees) for about 30 minutes or until golden brown.

Yield: 1 pie

Lindsay Speros
Washington

This was my grandmother's recipe. The pie is easy for teenagers to make.

"Rock-n-Roll" Ice Cream

3/4	cup milk
1	cup cream
1/3	cup sugar
1/2	teaspoon vanilla
	flavoring (chocolate, raspberry, etc.)
3/4	cup salt
	crushed ice
	1-pound and 3-pound empty coffee cans with lids
	masking tape

In the small can, mix the milk, cream, sugar, vanilla and flavoring. Place lid on can and tape it shut. Put the small can inside the large can. Pack the crushed ice around the edges of the small can. Sprinkle the salt over the ice. Put the lid on the large can and tape it shut. Roll the can back and forth with a friend for 10 to 15 minutes. Use your feet or your hands! Remove the small can from the large can. Open and you have homemade ice cream.

Way Jay Sermons
Washington

Sensational Snow Cream

Snow is a treat in our area. This recipe makes a snowy day even more fun!

1	cup sugar
1 1/2	cups milk
1	teaspoon vanilla
2	quarts snow

Mix sugar and milk well. Add vanilla and stir. Add snow and mix.

Matt and Beth Batchelor
Washington

Banana on a Stick

4   bananas (not mushy ones), peeled and halved
1   (12-ounce) bag chocolate chips
    popsicle sticks
    wax paper

Cover plate in wax paper. Cut the banana in half and push the popsicle stick into the bottom of the banana. Using a microwave or stove, melt chocolate chips. Stir constantly if on the stove; check every 15 seconds if using microwave. Roll the bananas in melted chocolate using a spoon to cover thoroughly. Place on plate covered with waxed paper, wrap with wax paper and freeze until the bananas are firm, approximately 2 hours.

Yield: 8 servings

Jeff Bennett
Washington

Even kids who aren't wild about bananas will love these!

Easy! Adult supervision needed.

Amazing Muffins

2 1/2 cups chocolate ice cream
1   cup (8-ounces) peanut butter chips
2   cups self-rising flour

Preheat oven to 400 degrees. Line a 12-cup muffin tin with paper baking cups. In a large bowl, stir the ice cream until very soft but not melted. Stir in the remaining ingredients until well blended. The mixture will be stiff. Fill each muffin cup about two-thirds full with batter. Bake for 18 to 20 minutes, or until wooden toothpick inserted in the center comes out clean. Let cool on a wire rack for about 5 minutes before serving.

Yield: 1 dozen muffins

Davis Lane Rumley
Washington

You can do a lot of experimenting with these muffins by using different ice cream flavors and mixing in ingredients such as white or chocolate chips, nuts and dried fruits.

Adults will have as much fun with this recipe as the children. The combinations are endless.

Monkey Bread

3	(8-ounce) cans refrigerated biscuit dough
1	cup sugar
1	teaspoon cinnamon
1/2	cup butter
1	cup brown sugar, firmly packed

Easy!

Preheat oven to 350 degrees. Separate biscuit dough pieces and cut each into 4 sections. Combine white sugar and cinnamon. Pour into brown paper bag, add biscuit pieces, a handful at a time, and shake to coat well. Layer pieces in greased and floured 10-inch tube pan. Melt butter. Blend in brown sugar and pour mixture over biscuit pieces. Bake for 20 minutes.

Yield: 12 servings

Aaron Sermons
Washington

Saturday Morning Pancakes

2	cups biscuit baking mix
1	cup milk
2	eggs
2	tablespoons lemon juice
4	teaspoons sugar
2	teaspoons cinnamon
1	teaspoon vanilla
	blueberries or crushed pineapple, optional

These are fun to make with your family on week-ends.

Easy! Adult supervision for younger children!

Mix all ingredients together with a wire whisk. Scoop desired amount into skillet. Flip when bubbles cover surface of pancake. Let cook until the underside is golden brown.

Yield: 4 servings

Alexandra Speros
Washington

Groovy Granola

1/2	cup oatmeal
1/8	cup cinnamon
1/4	cup sugar
1	cup crushed graham crackers
1/4	cup butter, melted

Mix together all ingredients. It's that easy!

Yield: 2 cups

This can be used as a topping for vanilla ice cream or frozen yogurt!

Ervin Lampert
Washington

Peanut Butter Playdough

1/2	cup peanut butter
1/2	cup honey
1/2	cup powdered milk

Knead ingredients until smooth. Let your child use as they would regular playdough. Chocolate chips, gumdrops, marshmallows, red hots or any other small candy is fun to use for eyes, ears, noses, hats, etc.

You can eat your creations!

Neill Jennings
Washington

Chocolate Clay

1	(10-ounce) bag of chocolate candy melts
1/3	cup white corn syrup
	plastic bag

Put chocolate into a bowl and microwave until melted. Stir in white corn syrup until it's the consistency of dough. Knead mixture over the sink until all liquid is squeezed out. Put the "clay" into the plastic bag and let it set for an hour. After an hour, you can mold it into fun shapes and silly creatures. Use your imagination.

You can make a chocolate rose by making lots of flat circles and wrapping them around a lollipop stick, which is the stem. Let it dry a little, and then it's ready to eat!

Emily Bennett
Washington

Spider Pretzels

These "spiders" look cute crawling on the table.

2   round crackers
2   teaspoons smooth peanut butter
4   small pretzel sticks
2   raisins

Spread peanut butter on one cracker and top with the other to make a sandwich. Insert 4 pretzel sticks on each side for legs. With a dab of peanut butter, put the two raisins on the top for eyes.

Yield: 1 spider

William Page
Washington

Stained Glass Lollipops

3   Lifesavers candy rolls
     aluminum foil
     cooking spray
10   popsicle or craft sticks for handles

Fun and easy. This must be done with an adult!

Spray small amount of cooking oil onto aluminum foil. Place 6 lifesavers in a circle, on the foil so they touch each other. Using an electric fry pan, slightly melt the lifesavers. Press a popsicle stick down into the warm lifesavers. Colors will blend together. Let cool. Remove from foil. Do not melt thoroughly or the lollipops will be too thin.

Yield: 10 lollipops

Jeff Bennett
Washington

Cookie Suckers

20	vanilla wafer cookies
1/2	cup peanut butter
1	(12-ounce) bag of semi-sweet chocolate chips
	container of multi-colored sprinkles
10	wooden craft (popsicle) sticks
	wax paper

Spread peanut butter on the flat side of each vanilla wafer. Place a craft stick into the peanut butter on 10 of the halves. Put the second peanut butter-coated cookie on the top of the one with the stick. The craft stick should be sandwiched between the halves and sticking out making it look like a cookie sucker. Place chocolate chips in a microwave safe bowl and melt (about 1 to 2 minutes) on high. Stir chips to make sure they are completely melted and smooth. Dip each cookie pop into chocolate and roll in sprinkles. Place on wax paper for a few minutes to cool.

Yield: 10 cookie pops

This works great using white chocolate as well. Red and green sprinkles are fun for Christmas, pink for Valentines, pastel sprinkles for Easter. There is no limit of variations for these treats!

Ferrell Sloan
Washington

Soup in a Jar

2/3	cup (3-ounce) dried cheese-filled tortellini
1/4	cup sun-dried tomatoes, snipped
1/3	cup dried split green peas
1/2	cup dried chopped carrots
1	tablespoon instant chicken bouillon granules
1	tablespoon dried minced onion
1/2	teaspoon dried basil, crushed
1/2	teaspoon dried thyme, crushed
1/2	teaspoon garlic powder
1/4	teaspoon ground pepper

Layer ingredients in a clean 1-pint glass canning jar in the following order from bottom to top: tortellini, dried tomatoes, split peas, carrots, and remaining seasonings. Cover jar and attach gift tag with directions for cooking.

Gift tag directions:

Empty jar ingredients into a 3-quart saucepan. Add 5 cups water. Bring mixture to a boil. Reduce heat; cover and simmer 50 minutes or until peas are tender. (Option: add 1 cup chopped cooked ham or sausage.)

Yield: 4 servings

Great teacher gift!

Emily Bennett
Washington

Mocha Mix

1 1/2 cups nonfat dry milk powder
1/3   cup brown sugar, firmly packed
1/2   cup instant coffee crystals
2/3   cup miniature semisweet chocolate pieces

Colorful Christmas mugs and ribbons create a special gift for friends and family.

In a medium mixing bowl, mix all ingredients well. Divide mixture into three gift containers. Seal containers. Attach gift tag with the following instructions:

Pour 2/3 cup boiling water in a blender container. Add 1/4 cup of the mix. Cover tightly. Blend until well combined and frothy. Pour into a mug and enjoy.

Yield: three 1-cup gifts

Reed Padgett
Washington

Holiday Jar Cookies

1/4   cup sugar
1/2   cup brown sugar, packed
1 1/2 cups all-purpose flour
3/4   teaspoon baking soda
1/4   teaspoon baking powder
1/2   cup holiday M&Ms
1/2   cup rolled oats
1/2   cup cocoa or regular crisped-rice cereal
1/2   cup white chocolate chips

This makes a festive holiday gift for the cooks on your list.

In a 1-quart jar, layer the above ingredients in the order listed, packing each layer firmly with a wooden spoon. Screw on the lid and prepare a gift tag with the following instructions:

To make your jar cookies, cream together 1/2 cup butter, 1/2 teaspoon vanilla and 1 egg in a large bowl. Add the contents of the jar and stir until well blended. Drop by rounded teaspoonfuls onto an ungreased cookie sheet. Bake at 350 degrees for 10 to 12 minutes.

Yield: 4 dozen

Anna Lane Mayo
Washington Park

Koolaid Playdough

1   cup all-purpose flour
1/2   cup salt
2   teaspoons cream of tartar
1   package unsweetened Koolaid
1   cup boiling water
1   tablespoon vegetable oil

Stir first 4 ingredients together until a soft dough forms. Knead until smooth. Add water and vegetable oil. Store in an air-tight container.

Josh Padgett
Washington

Bright colors and wonderful smells created by the Koolaid makes this playdough irresistible!

Baker's Clay

4   cups all-purpose flour
1   cup salt
1 1/4
  to 1 1/2 cups water

Combine all ingredients and knead until smooth. Use cookie cutters and make shapes. Bake at 300 degrees for 30 to 45 minutes. Watch carefully for color change. Golden means they're done. Remove from oven. Cool. Paint with acrylic and seal with a coat of shellac after paint dries.

Anna Lane Mayo
Washington Park

Great to use for ornaments at Christmas!

Homemade Soap

1 3/4 cups Ivory Snow soap powder
1/4   cup water
60   drops food coloring
        small plastic mold (or ice cube trays work well)

Mix together soap powder and water. Add food coloring and stir into paste consistency. Pour into molds and leave for several days to harden. Remove from molds. Let sit for three more days before using.

Jack May
Washington

Wrap up several chunks of soap in a cute soapdish and give to grandparents!

Patrick's Face Paint

Muffin tins work well for holding face paint.

1   teaspoon cornstarch
1/2   teaspoon water
1/2   teaspoon cold cream
         food coloring
         small empty yogurt container, clean and dry (1 for each color of paint)
         small paintbrushes

Stir together cornstarch and cold cream until well-blended. Add water and stir. Add food coloring, one drop at a time until you get the color you like. Experiment with the colors by adding more drops of the same color for a darker paint or by adding a different color to create a new shade. Paint designs on faces with a small paint-brush. Remove with soap and water.

Patrick Mayo
Washington Park

Sydney's Finger Paints

3   tablespoons sugar
1/2   cup cornstarch
2   cups cold water
         food coloring (variety of colors)
         soap flakes or liquid dishwashing detergent
         medium-sized saucepan
         muffin tin or 4 to 5 small cups

Mix sugar and cornstarch together in a medium saucepan over low heat. Add cold water and continue stirring until the mixture is thick. Remove from heat. Divide the mixture up into 4 to 5 portions, spooning them into sections of a muffin tin or small cups. Add a drop or two of food coloring and a pinch of soap flakes or dish detergent to each portion. A different color should be used for each cup. Stir and let cool.

Sydney Edwards
Washington

Glorious Gak

4	ounces white glue
4	ounces water
	a good squeeze of poster paint or washable paint

Mix these ingredients together in a bowl.

1/2	cup water
3/4	teaspoon borax powder

Mix these together in a different bowl.

Combine the borax mixture into the glue mixture and the fun begins!

Ferrell Sloan
Washington

This is so much fun to do for a class party. The children love it! Change colors for different holidays.

The Best Bubbles

1	cup liquid dishwashing detergent
2	cups warm water
3 to 4	tablespoons glycerine (found at drug stores)
1	teaspoon sugar
	large plastic container
	"Found" bubble makers

Gently stir all ingredients together in a big plastic container. Look around your house for things that will make good bubbles, like cookie cutters, paper cups, straws or funnels. Dip your bubble makers into the brew and either blow through them or wave them in the air. If you want to save your bubble brew for another time, cover the container with a tight fitting lid and store.

Tap Perry
Washington

Bubbles work best when the humidity is high.

Crystal Garden

An old favorite!

4   tablespoons salt
4   tablespoons water
1   tablespoon ammonia
**   charcoal**
**   colored inks (cartridge pen refills work well; punch a small hole in one**
**   end and squeeze)**

Mix together salt, water and ammonia. Pour mixture over several small pieces of charcoal in a small bowl. Put a few drops of different colored inks on various parts of the charcoal. Leave undisturbed for several days, and crystals will grow and cover the charcoal in interesting formations, developing and spreading everyday. The crystals will be white where no ink is used.

Liza Page
Washington

Homemade "Silly Putty"

1   part Elmer's school glue gel (must be gel)
1   part liquid laundry starch
**   store-purchased plastic Easter eggs**

Measure equal parts of glue and starch and pour into a bowl and mix. As product begins to thicken, knead until thoroughly mixed. Divide into 1 to 1 1/2-inch balls and store in plastic Easter eggs.

Caleb Asby
Aurora

The Cookbook Committee wishes to thank our members, families, friends and fellow Beaufort County residents for submitting their treasured recipes and steadfastly supporting the development of this cookbook. We are truly grateful to all these individuals who contributed so generously to *Plate & Palette.*

Adams, Katherine
Alligood, Charlene
Asby, Caleb
Ashburn, Emily M.
Baade, Mary
Batchelor, Matt and Beth
Bateman, Charles
Beach, Lorrie
Bell, Laura
Bennett, Emily
Bennett, Jeff
Bergevin, Terri
Bonner, Frank
Bonner, Grace
Bonner, Helen
Boyer, Linda
Bright, Louise
Brothers, Thora
Buckman, Etta
Buckman, Mildred
Burbage, Barbara
Burkart, Pamela Gunnin
Campbell, Jay
Campbell, Joan
Carter, Tay
Carver, Elsie Lois
Cayton, Ramona
Champion, Gale
Chapin, Mary Alice
Cheshire, Lucy
Clark, Alex and Tyler
Collier, Beth
Collier, Hawes and Beck
Collis, Nancy
Conlon, Joan
Cooper, Athy
Crawford, Kara and Mike
Daniel, F. Harry
Davidson, Priscilla
Davis, Doug
De Hoog, Jan
De Hoog, Nancy
Deans, Michael
Deans, Steven
Dicken, Betty Anne
Dorn, Margaret
Douglas, Alva
Edwards, Rosemarie
Edwards, Ruth
Edwards, Sydney
Edwards, Tatum
Edwards, Tori
Elks, Alice C.
Encinias, Phyllis
Evans, Sylvia
Fentress, Gloria
Fields, Jane
Forbes, Irene
Fowle, Frannye
Fowle, Sadie
Francisco, Barbara
Furlough, Nancy B.
Futrell, Rachel

Galuszka, Doris Miller
Geis, Diane
Glass, Karen
Gorham, Burkely
Graves, Lind
Graves, Sue
Gray, Betty Mitchell
Griffin, Nora Mae
Grimes, Lily G.
Harrington, Ann Bryan
Harris, Corry T.
Harvey, Sandra
Harvey, Shields
Hatala, Mary Jo
Hawkins, Nan
Hill, Pat
Hindsley, Dr. Pack
Hodges, Jane
Hodges, Kack
Hoell, Herbert
Hoell, Julie
Hollowell, Lou
Holmes, Elizabeth
Hooker, Lillian V.
Hopkins, Lillian W.
Hopkins, Ruth
Howard, Connie
Huber, Johanna and Leonard
Hudson, Peggy
Hulbert, Frances
Hull, Mary C.
Israel, Jan
Ives, Jean
Jackson, Christine
Jenkins, Jaye
Jennings, Archie
Jennings, Lydie
Jennings, Neill
Jennings, Sarah
Johnson, Wanda
Jones, Hansy
Kidd, Hester Anne
Kidwell, Judy
Knott, Terry
Kuiken, Agnes
Lampert, Ervin
Lane, Louise
Larkin, Frances
Lassiter, Frances
Lassiter, Hazel
Leach, Katirie
Lee, Jean Gerard
Leiner, Marion
Lewis, Judy
Lilley, Nancy J.
Mansfield, Sue
May, Daniel
May, Jack
Mayer, Kaye
Mayne, Emily
Mayo, Anna Lane
Mayo, Patrick
McClure, Alice

McDonough, Juliette
McRoy, Martha
Meier, Flo
Mers, Peggy
Miller, Linda C.
Mills, Phebie
Moore, Joyce W.
Moore, Mary Emily
Morgan, Ellen
Morgan, Gayle
Murray, Gray
Murray, Madison and Sam
Murray, Nancy
Myers, Helen
Nash, Carol
Nash, David
Nash, Nancy H.
Nicholson, Sue
Niederbuehl, Linda
Norman, Alice
Nunnally, Kathryn
O'Neal, Harriet W.
Padgett, Josh
Padgett, Reed
Padgett, Shirley
Page, Beth
Page, Jane
Page, Janie
Page, Liza
Page, William
Partrick, Catherine
Paulson, Mary
Payne, Mary W.
Peele, Marella and Ben
Peele, Mavis Rodman
Perry, Tap
Peters, Ann
Phillips, Carly
Phillips, Dr. Tom
Phillips, Joe
Potter, Carmen Alen
Potter, Richard
Potts, Robin
Pugh, Ruth
Pyburn, Cathy
Pyburn, Leah
Rios, Marcus
Robbins, Betsy
Roberson, Frances Morgan
Robinson, Jingle
Ross, Lib
Roth, Marilyn
Rumley, Anne Stuart
Rumley, Davis Lane
Rumley, Jeff
Rumley, Mildred
Sandy, Maxine C.
Scales, Sallie
Schramm, Ethel
Seale, Linda
Seale, Richard
Sermons, Aaron
Sermons, Lynn

Sermons, Jr., Wayland J.
Sermons, Way Jay
Sharpe, Kay
Shook, Jean
Simmons, Bea
Sloan, Beth
Sloan, Ferrell
Sloan, Lewis
Sloan, Jr., Lewis
Sloan, Sarah
Smith, Barbara Ann
Smith, Dottie Lou
Smith, Melba G. -
    River Forest Manor
Smith, Vance
Smithwick, Laura T.
Smyre, Nannette
Sommerkamp, Helen
Sparrow, Jan
Sparrow, Marguerite
Speros, Alexandra
Speros, Dr. Tom
Speros, Lindsay
Stephenson, Frances
Stewart, Virgil
Talley, Tucker
Tankard, Wayne
Tate, Dolores M.
Tate, John
Tate, Katherine Howdy
Tate, William
Taylor, Kathleen
Tetterton, Rita P.
Tigchelaar, Gerda
Trainer, Margaret Sloan
Tranters Creek Herring Club
Tripp, Evelyn L.
Trueblood, Jean Duke
Tubaugh, Betty
Tucker, Roy
Tunstall, Emily Bryan
Upton, Lexa
Valdez, Daniel and A.J.
Valdez, Dannielle
Van Camp, Vera
Van Dorp, Hank
Van Essendelft, Elenore
Van Staalduinen, Ann
Van Staalduinen, Jeanne
Vann, Lee M.
Wells, Wilma
Whichard, Cathy
Whitley, Audrey
Wiley, Edna
Williams, Mary Catherine
Wilson, Mary
Windley, Ann
Winfrey, Nancy
Wiseman, Ann and Ray
Woods, Ruby Lee
Woolard, Margaret
Woolridge, Roberta

 Index

 Index

Index

R

S

Index

Beaufort County Arts Council

108 Gladden Street
P.O. Box 634
Washington, NC 27889
252-946-2504
e-mail: beauxarts@coastalnet.com
website: www.beaufortcountyartscouncil.org

Please send me _____ copies of **Plate & Palette**   @ $25.00 each   _____
(tax included)

Postage and Handling   @   5.00 each   _____

                                                    Total   _____

Name _____

Address _____

City _____ State _____ Zip _____

Daytime Phone _____

Make checks payable to the Beaufort County Arts Council

Beaufort County Arts Council

108 Gladden Street
P.O. Box 634
Washington, NC 27889
252-946-2504
e-mail: beauxarts@coastalnet.com
website: www.beaufortcountyartscouncil.org

Please send me _____ copies of **Plate & Palette**   @ $25.00 each   _____
(tax included)

Postage and Handling   @   5.00 each   _____

                                                    Total   _____

Name _____

Address _____

City _____ State _____ Zip _____

Daytime Phone _____

Make checks payable to the Beaufort County Arts Council